THE WORD

THE
WORD

Guiding Principles for Everyday Living

Dr. Lola B. Allen

First published in Jamaica 2013 by
Lola B. Allen
Kingston, Jamaica W.I.
Email: lbaword@cwjamaica.com

©2013 by Lola B. Allen

All rights reserved. No part of this publication may be reproduced, stored, in a retrieval system or transmitted in any form or by any means electronic, mechanical, photocopying, recording or otherwise, without the prior written permission of the publisher and author.

A catalogue record of this book is available
from the National Library of Jamaica.

ISBN 978-976-954-631-8

Available also in e-book versions

Scripture quotations in this book are from the
New King James version (NKJV).

©1982 by Thomas Nelson, Inc.
Used by permission all rights reserved.
Other quotations from the King James version are
denoted as, (KJV) unless stated otherwise.
Definitions used in this book are from *The Little Oxford Dictionary &
Thesaurus*, revised edition. ©1998 by Oxford University Press.

Cover and book design by Robert Harris
Set in Californian Text 11.5/15.5
Printed in Jamaica.

"By the word of the Lord the heavens were made;
and all the host of them by the breath of his mouth."
~ Psalm 33:6 (KJV)

Part I: Guiding Principles, is dedicated to
my daughter, Anabelle.
Thank you, Anabelle, for your questions and comments.
You have been a source of inspiration.
Continue to shine for God. Love always.
Mum

Contents

Preface / *xi*

Acknowledgements / *xiii*

PART I: GUIDING PRINCIPLES

1   Introduction / *1*
2   Reading / *3*
3   Believing / *7*
4   Relationship Building / *20*
5   Faith / *42*
6   Overcoming Challenges / *53*
7   Covetousness / *78*
8   Anger / *90*
9   Pride / *98*
10   Humility / *104*
11   Patience / *112*
12   Nature's Lesson on Patience, Humility and Pride and Valuable Lessons on Driving / *119*
13   Discontentment / *125*
14   Attitude / *135*
15   Unforgiveness / *144*

CONTENTS

16	Thanksgiving	/ 156
17	Giving	/ 161
18	Idolatry	/ 177
19	Religion	/ 182
20	Timely Reminders	/ 193
21	Conclusion	/ 199

PART II: GOD'S PLAN OF SALVATION
(From Creation to Eternity)

22	Introduction	/ 208
23	Knowing God	/ 211
24	The Unchanging God	/ 214
25	The Master Creator	/ 218
26	Life Giving	/ 220
27	The Blinding Effects of Sin	/ 224
28	The Forerunner	/ 228
29	The Chosen Witness	/ 231
30	Accepting Your Role	/ 234
31	Identifying The True Light	/ 237
32	The Mystery of The Father and The Son	/ 241
33	Rejection	/ 245
34	Becoming Heirs	/ 249
35	Spiritual Rebirth	/ 252
36	Conclusion	/ 255

Preface

The use of words is the universal manner in which we as human beings communicate with each other. When we attempt to communicate with persons who speak a different language from us, communication is not usually effective. Effective communication is therefore needed to ensure that the message sent is understood by the receiver. If necessary a translator can be used to overcome language barriers which prevent understanding. Sign language and body language are other means of communication used to express unspoken words.

Words are important in our family relationships with our children and partners. A baby's cry can be translated into words to express hunger or some other discomfort. Some other ways in which we use words are in our relationship with our employers, our friends and our church communities. Examples of what might be discussed in each of the aforementioned groups include: organizational goals, sharing secrets and spreading the gospel respectively.

Governments in our societies use words too when they govern using laws and by-laws. Words, therefore, allow us to interact with each other in every facet of life. Where did the use of words originate? In the beginning; God spoke and the

PREFACE

heaven and earth came into being. From the time of creation until now God continues to use words whether spoken through the Holy Bible, His prophets, His pastors and other human beings. God also speaks to us through nature. The ants denote industry by storing food before it is needed and the plumage of the peacock denotes elegance, all unspoken words.

Given the many ways in which words are used, one of the questions you might ask is: how are God's words significant in our daily lives in today's society? This book is written in two parts and the introduction in each part briefly explains the significance of God's words in our lives. Parts I and II of this book will leave you so excited that you will immediately want to make changes to your life where necessary or be encouraged to reinforce aspects of your life that you know are pleasing to God. Please read *The Word: Guiding Principles for Everyday Living* and be blessed.

Acknowledgements

Thanks to my typist Mark Taylor. I thank God for the gift He has given to you which enabled you to decipher my mostly illegible hand writing.

My typing skills were tested when Mark, due to prior commitment was unable to type Part II. God knew that I needed help and so He sent Thelma Thomas to complete the typing. Thank you Thelma, your assistance was divinely ordained. Thank you, God.

Thanks also to Mark Taylor, my dear friend, Jacqueline Wilson and my daughter, Anabelle for helping me to meet the deadline in the 'amateur' proof reading of the first draft of the book. It was hard work and somewhat frustrating at times but our prayers were answered as God gave us the strength.

Mrs. Barbara Jekir, proof reader, and Miss Kristina Exell, editor, thank you both for your many suggestions.

Thank you God for sparing my life and giving me this opportunity to use the many and varied experiences you have provided in my life, talents and vision that have all been so invaluable in the writing of this book.

Lord, how could I forget the lessons you provided in patience and perseverance when I spent days and nights tirelessly re-typing pages with errors. It was difficult while the

ACKNOWLEDGEMENTS

experience lasted. Now looking back I want to say 'Thank you Lord, You are awesome'. I never believed that day would come when the task would be completed. I now understand what it means to be patient in tribulation.

Finally, as an act of faith, I want to thank God for the millions of lives locally and internationally that will be transformed through this book.

To God be the glory.

– PART I –

GUIDING PRINCIPLES

How will I know right from wrong without a guide?

"Your word is a lamp to my feet and a light to my path".
Psalm 119:105

– 1 –

Introduction

Secular life is guided by rules, laws, "do's and don'ts" (often described as societal norms) that guide our actions to ensure that our society becomes more orderly. If you break the speed limit you pay a fine and if you own property you are expected to pay property tax. These two examples demonstrate ways in which laws impact our lives.

Similarly, God has provided for us spiritual guidelines or principles that will help us to live happily here on earth as well as enable us to benefit from His gift of eternal life ultimately.

In Part 1 of this book, I have used simple everyday examples to highlight the importance of these guiding principles.

I find that for one reason or another reading is not usually on our priority list and I have used chapter 2 to highlight its importance. Reading plays a vital role in our personal growth and development and I am sure that you all agree with me on this. In chapter 2, I have elaborated on the importance of reading to garner knowledge as opposed to just listening to others express their opinion.

God encourages reading as a source of relevant and vital

information and this is demonstrated in His command to Joshua:

> "The Book of The Law shall not depart from your mouth, but you shall meditate in it day and night, that you may observe to do according to all that is written in it. For then you will make your way prosperous, and then you will have good success."
>
> ~ Joshua 1: 8 (KJV)

Please note, in the aforementioned passage God says all that is written. This means that you will have to read in order to know what God expects of you. When you read you will also understand the importance of being obedient to Him.

After completing the introduction and the chapter on reading, I know you will be eager to discover the content of the other chapters.

I hope that Part I of this book will provide clarity, reinforce some truths or even give you a new perspective on these guiding principles that will be life transforming.

− 2 −

Reading

Your question regarding this chapter on reading might be, 'Why write a book and include a chapter on reading?' You might even go further to ask a second question, 'Why write the book if you believe it will not be read?' I understand the rationale that would have resulted in your need to ask these two questions. I hope that this chapter will provide the answers. Now it is my turn to ask you one vital question: Do you read all the books that you purchase?

I anticipate your response to my question, the answer is simply no. We are all guilty (and that includes me) of not reading all the books we purchase. Many persons will confess that these books are in their study, the car, on the night table, at the office and ....

....

(Include other places in the space provided) but somehow they have not found the time to read.

This is an opportune time to share with you the importance of reading. When you read you are able to get your own perspective on or understanding of the content of a book. Reading provides an opportunity for exploration as you are able to browse the internet, discuss your views with a friend, lecturer, your minister and other persons you believe might provide some intellectual stimulation to increase your knowledge. Exploration provides answers which also guides you into a better understanding of the relevance of what has been read generally and, where applicable foster growth in your life.

There is no growth or intellectual stimulation when books remain unopened. The only thing that is likely to happen is the accumulation of dust, on a valuable source of knowledge.

Technology has helped to make our lives much easier. We should now be all eager to do some form of reading as the internet is here to help us garner information which includes our unanswered questions that we might not want others to help us with. Thanks to the search engines............................
....
(Include these in the space provided). Information is now available to us at our convenience and the world would not know that we needed help.

You need to remember that listening to another person's perspective on a book is providing you with the individual's understanding of the material read. If you do not read for yourself, then you will only be using that person's perspective to guide your thought process. If that person's opinion is subjective or if he or she misinterprets the author's ideas, you would never know, unless you deem reading to be an important part of your intellectual growth and do your personal reading.

You have been blessed by God with the ability to read, so please read for yourself and determine if your opinion is similar

READING

to or different from others. Where there are differences, challenge others by asking them questions which will help you to endorse or change your views as you deem necessary based on what you have read.

Let us do some exploration to substantiate the importance of reading. If you go to school and do not read your text book, you would never know if what your teacher has taught you is factual or if it is his or her opinion. Similarly, if you do not read as a part of your preparation for your examination, you are likely to fail. On the other hand, if you read and do not understand but refuse to ask questions to seek clarity, you would also fail.

Reading is a stimulant of the mind when, questions are asked, comparisons are made, differences are highlighted and conclusions drawn. In other words, as one reads one should reason as this skill is developed with practice.

There are a number of persons who are selective readers. Some of these persons read in order to be successful in high school, college or university and will read only the books that are needed to pass their examinations and nothing else. I want to remind these persons that life does not end with passing examinations and getting a job based on the examination results. There are other persons who will read the newspapers or magazines to keep abreast with local and international affairs but will not read anything else.

Others will read science fiction and some of us will read other things based on our personal interest, which could include, gardening, tennis, cooking ....
....
(Include your taste). Finally, there are others who will have to

be cajoled into reading (If you fall into this category, please read this chapter twice).

I encourage you to read more to widen your knowledge base. God wants us to be informed as much as possible about things that are a part of this world including the spiritual facet that will determine our place in eternity and so He wants us to read, to learn and to grow.

Reading provides the solid foundation needed to enhance our intellectual and spiritual growth as we learn more about God through reading of the Holy Bible along with other inspirational books.

In these times, we are beset by so many trials and sometimes these occur when we least expect. There are times when these trials occur and we might not even have the time to call a friend to get a word of encouragement. However, if we make it a habit to read God's Word we will be able to recall words that will provide some form of comfort that will be relevant to the trial being experienced.

– 3 –

Believing

What comes to your mind when you think about the word, believing? The first thing that comes to my mind is the father, mentioned in the Bible, in Mark chapter 9, who had asked Jesus to have compassion and heal his son of the mute spirit:

> *Jesus said to him, "If thou can believe, all things are possible to him who believes." Immediately the father of the child cried out and said with tears, "Lord, I believe; help my unbelief!"*
>
> *~ Mark 9: 23-24*

This father's response gives us a clear picture of how difficult it is to believe. In my own words, this father was saying to Jesus: "Lord, I really want to believe in you and your power to perform miracles. I must confess that the things you can do are difficult for me to accept as a human being. Lord, human beings cannot perform miracles and so I am not accustomed to seeing these miracles performed around me on a daily basis as you have been doing. Mentally, I have to adjust to this new experience for it is too much for my human mind to process and accept. However, Lord, if you help me to get to that place of complete trust in you and in your power, I know I will believe."

Can you identify with anything I have said in my attempt at paraphrasing the father's honesty to Jesus?

So far my discourse about this father should provide an understanding of the meaning of the word belief. Is there a consensus on this? Let us now formalize the meaning of believing then relate it to the Word of God. Believing is defined by *The Little Oxford Dictionary and Thesaurus* as accepting as true what is said or done.

When you believe that God is real that He is not a figment or a myth but that He exists and works in a mysterious way, then you will have learnt to trust God completely.

To demonstrate the importance of believing when we pray Jesus said:

"And whatever things you ask in prayer, believing, you will receive."

~ Matthew 21:22

I must confess, that being human, sometimes I am really baffled by the things that God has done and continues to do. I have learnt, however, to accept that our God is an awesome God and that you and I cannot and will never be able to rationalize or explain the power of God and so I humbly believe. One thing is irrefutable and that is, the evidence of God's power abounds in this universe. Just look at some of the things in God's creation: the beautiful birds, flowers, the mountains and the water falls. God's power is amazing and I stand in awe at the beauty of the ocean with all the sea creatures and plants (that I see on cable television as I cannot

swim). Include some of the things that fascinate you in God's creation in the space provided...................................
....

Have you ever watched the waves from the sea shore how they appear to be coming head on at you and then suddenly they recede? It is amazing the control God exercises over the waves:

"You rule the raging of the sea; when its waves rise, You still them."

~ Psalm 89:9-10

The list of what God has created is endless . . . . Do you believe in God now? Here is another opportunity to believe:

Have you ever stopped to take a look in the mirror at how beautiful you are and at the unique physique that God has given to you? (Why are you looking around or thinking about others?)

Please pause now, go and look in the mirror for confirmation concerning what I just said. Do not allow the world to trap you into believing that there is a standard look that defines beauty and if you do not meet the criteria you are not beautiful. Any statement of this nature is a big joke.

You are not a copy; you are an original and therefore you are uniquely beautiful.

Your only comparison is with the image of God, in which you were created and not with your fellow human beings:

"So God created man in His own image; in the image of God he created him; male and female He created them."

~ Genesis 1:27

THE WORD

Do you see how special we are to God? He has made us in His image. David expressed his gratitude to God for the way he was made:

> *"I will praise You, for I am fearfully and wonderfully made; marvelous are your works and that my soul knows very well."*
>
> ~ *Psalm 139:14*

I hope that by this you would have believed that you are beautiful and are made in the image of God. Let us now look at some other reasons that should make it easy for us to believe.

In the Bible, Jesus forewarned us of some things that would happen in the last days. Even as I am writing this book some of these things are occurring:

> *"And you will hear of wars and rumors of wars. See that you are not troubled; for all these things must come to pass, but the end is not yet."*
>
> ~ *Matthew 24:6*

What are you learning about these times from magazines, newspapers, the internet and other sources, about wars? (Some persons might be living in places right now where war is a part of their daily lives). Yes! There are wars occurring and there are also rumors of wars as Jesus predicted.

Have you experienced or heard about natural disasters and nations that are rising against each other. Again, Jesus prepared us for these times:

> *"For nation will rise against nation, and kingdom against kingdom. And there will be famines, pestilences and earthquakes in various places."*
>
> ~ *Matthew 24:7*

Some of you might be saying, "These occurrences are not unusual as throughout history there have always been wars, rumors of wars, earthquakes and other natural disasters."

I agree with you, good point. However, I am sure you will agree that these disasters are now occurring more frequently and on a magnitude not previously experienced.

God has prepared us for these times in His Word, the Holy Bible and whether we choose to believe or have elements of doubt these things will continue to occur.

Have you ever thought about the many tribulations that beset humanity in these times? These did not occur without warning from Jesus:

"For then there will be great tribulation, such as has not been since the beginning of the world until this time, no nor ever shall be."

~ Matthew 24:21

In my own words, God is saying to us that humanity will face challenging times that will be unmatched. We have never faced these challenges before and will never face such challenges again after this period.

Isn't this another opportunity to believe God?

What about the speed at which times passes daily? My dear readers, am I the only one who feels like I am racing just to keep up with my daily activities because time is moving swiftly? When I wake up in the morning and look at the clock it is usually 5:00 am. I usually say out loud, "I'll enjoy lazing in bed for ten more minutes." My next glance at the clock is always a big surprise as it is usually 6:00 am or 6:10 am. Whether or not I want to believe it one hour or more has passed which feels like five or ten minutes.

Can you identify with my experience with the speed of time? Isn't it really frightening? Sometimes I look around to see if someone pulled a fast one on me and fast forwarded the hands of the clock. To date I have not been able to catch anyone in the act. I won't either; it is God at work, He is awesome.

The speed of time is another way God chooses to demonstrate His power and we have no choice but to accept this. If we do not accept that God is in control of time, we will lead frustrated lives trying to prove that we can get everything done on time without God's guidance and this is not possible. What will happen instead is that we will all get stressed out and eventually pay the price with our health.

Please s-l-o-w down and ask for God's guidance. I remember some years ago I saw a poster which read "It is better to be late in this world than to be too early in the next."

Please do not go to the other extreme and blame me for using scare tactics by my reference to the poster on the possibility of a 'premature death' ('to be too early in the next world'). If you do, this could result in slowing down your actions almost to a halt in your life. You really do not want your performance to be substandard. Ensure that all your projects, reports, arrival at work, school, church or other engagements are done on time.

Let me reiterate the point on the usage of time:

We need to ask God to help us to manage our time so that we can achieve our objectives. This will prevent us from becoming flustered, help us to lead balanced lives which include periods of rest, relaxation and time for spiritual growth. This balanced lifestyle will help to reduce our stress level and prevent us from going to the grave earlier than God intended.

BELIEVING

When you become overwhelmed by life's activities and take your eyes off Jesus, the scripture below will remind you that God is in control:

> *"Trust in the Lord with all your heart, and lean not on your own understanding; In all your ways acknowledge Him and He shall direct your path."*
>
> *Proverbs 3: 5–6*

I will give you a few minutes break to memorize the passage above. For me the real test of the speed at which time goes by these days is when I make a comparison with what happened in my adolescent years. As a teenager in high school I wondered if the first five years would ever end. Time "[way ←back]" then seemed to have gone by s-l-o-w-l-y. Can you identify with my experience then? Teenagers and young adults living in this period would not be able to identify with my experience since time is now moving at an accelerated pace.

We can thank God again! For He has provided another opportunity for us to believe based on His Word relating to the speed of time:

> *"And unless the Lord had shortened those days, no flesh would be saved; but for the elect's sake, whom He chose He shortened the days."*
>
> *~ Mark 13:20*

We should all be grateful for the elect for whose benefit God has chosen to shorten the days.

Imagine what it would be like with all that is happening in our world today: natural disasters . . . crime and violence . . . price increases . . . diseases . . . famine and with time, just d-r-a-g-g-i-n-g. In other words, time would be moving at the pace it did in my adolescent years, slowly not swiftly. Do you get a clear picture of what life would be like if we face all these things in slow motion? It would be sheer torture. I have used God's Word to demonstrate what is happening in our world today and the importance of relying on His Word as our guide. If we believe, it is easier to cope and if we doubt we are more likely to become frustrated.

I know it is not always easy to believe God as He is a Spirit and we cannot see Him or touch Him.

It is important, however to look at His Word, His world and all His works in the universe which are all reminders that God never fails.

As humans we tend to believe the things we are told by our fellow human beings. There are so many times when they disappoint us by not being totally honest but yet we still find it easier to trust them. On the other hand, God who cannot lie is doubted. Let's use God's Word to substantiate this fact:

> *"God is not a man, that He should lie, nor a son of man, that He should repent. Has He said and will He not do? Or has He said and will He not make it good?"*
>
> *~ Numbers 23: 19*

There are many persons who doubt God's plan of salvation and scoff at His gift of eternal life which they see as impossible. Please read the passage below:

> *"In hope of eternal life which God, who cannot lie, promised before time began."*
>
> *~ Titus 1:2*

BELIEVING

My dear readers, eternity is real. You can spend it with Jesus or spend it in hell where there is eternal punishment . . . it goes on f-o-r-e-v-e-r. There is one thing I ask of you, please do not live in denial or allow anyone to trick you into believing that when you die, all that follows is the wake, funeral service and eventually the body decays and it all ends there. For those who think once the body is cremated there won't be another burning of the body in hell, if your life isn't pleasing to God, then I am sorry to disappoint you. God, your creator, has the power to bring you back to His original creation to face judgment (Revelation 20: 11–5).

Read also Ezekiel chapter 37 and you will see the power of God in bringing back to life an exceedingly great army from the valley of dry bones. Stop now and read the chapter; it will eliminate any doubts you might have had about the power of God in bringing back to life all the persons that have died, even the ones eaten by wild animals, sharks and those drowned whose bodies have never been found.

Let us now take it step by step and examine together the passages below that will provide clarity once and for all on the worms (that destroy the body), fire (relating to eternity for those who disobey God), eternal life for those who obey God and the power of God to restore our bodies for judgement which includes embalmed bodies and charred remains. Are you now attuned with reality, that there is no escape from facing up to judgement? I want you to be like me and admit that it is frightening. However, we all have an option that has a favourable outcome to enjoy eternal life when we are obedient to God.

Starting with the worms that destroy the decaying body read along with me what Job said:

THE WORD

And though after my skin worms destroy this body, yet in my flesh will I see God.

~ Job 19: 26 (KJV)

Now let us pause . . . Job is saying that worms will destroy his body. However, He did not end there as he went on to say he would see God in his flesh. This confirms God's power in bringing us back to His original creation to face judgement whether the body was cremated, embalmed or otherwise.

Mark chapter 9 provides sound advice to us as to how to avoid hell's fire. Mark suggests to us that it would be better to lose a member of our body that would result in us sinning rather than to have all our members intact and end up in hell's fire. He further illustrates the point using the hand, foot and eye (which reminds us to be careful with what we do, where we go and what we see respectively) as examples of parts of the body that we should be willing to dismember rather than sacrifice our place in eternity with God. Let us now look at what Mark says in the Bible:

If your hand causes you to sin, cut it off. It is better for you to enter into life maimed, rather than having two hands, to go to hell, into the fire that shall never be quenched – where their worm does not die and the fire is not quenched.

~ Mark 9:43–44

If you were reading along with me you would note that twice Mark mentioned the fact that there is no quenching of the fire in hell. Just in case we might all think that the fire might burn out like the ones we sometimes light here on earth Mark makes it explicit; the fire shall never be quenched.

For emphasis Mark wants us to understand that the punishment is a 'packaged deal', fire that is not quenched and worms that never die both coming at your flesh simultaneously. I certainly by the grace of God will do everything to avoid hell's fire. I do not even like to see a worm crawling near to me let alone having worms cover my flesh and have a feast with me watching them, feeling them, being burnt and there being no escape . . . I don't even know what to say. 'A terrifying experience' are the only words that come to my mind and that is an understatement.

Your reading assignment, to be done now, is to find out what Mark said about the eye and foot in Mark 9: 45–48.

We had a graphic description of what the everlasting fire will be like from Mark.

Matthew reinforced the point that our lifestyle will determine our eternal status:

And these will go away into everlasting punishment (persons who are disobedient), but the righteous into eternal life (persons who are obedient).

~ Matthew 25:46

I pray that you and I will be included among those called by Jesus to inherit the kingdom prepared for those who are obedient.

The point cannot be overemphasized that obedience to God is the path we should all take.

In addition, I have provided you with adequate evidence to substantiate the importance of believing so that you can live your life confidently knowing that you will have a place with Jesus.

THE WORD

Do not allow your doubts to be a deterrent to believing in Jesus. As human beings we all have the capacity to believe. It is expected, we will all have moments of doubt like the father whose son had the mute spirit in Mark chapter 9. You, too, should be like that father who honestly expressed his doubts to Jesus about believing. You need to tell Jesus not only about your doubts but that you really want to believe Him with all your heart. Jesus will help you to get to that place of complete trust. You have everything to gain by being honest with Jesus and you will lose everything worth having which includes joy, peace and eternal life if you do not reach out and accept Jesus' invitation. Remember, Jesus never fails.

If you make the choice to harden your heart and not believe in God, you will only have yourself to blame for this. Never forget that God has given you free will which enables you to make your own choice. Reference will be made where necessary throughout the book to the wrong choice made by Adam and Eve resulting in sin and suffering in the world. Read more about this in Genesis chapter 3.

If you believe, please join me in saying, "God is real, He is faithful and He never lies." I am confident that many persons believe God and have joined me in acknowledging His goodness.

Welcome to an exciting life in believing God! Please note, you will face trials, things might not work out as planned, you may experience redundancy, foreclosure or other unexpected challenges..

....

(Include your challenge(s) in the space provided). You will learn through these experiences that God loves you and has a plan for you. Even in these negative circumstances Jesus is working for your good.

I have said enough on believing. If you really understand the importance of it in your relationship with God, please complete the line below:

I _____ do believe in God and His Word.
      Your Name

Remember the words of Jesus:

"If you can believe all things are possible to him who believes.

~ Mark 9:23

Believe and experience God's goodness.

– 4 –

Relationship Building

Relationship building takes time; it does not happen overnight. As human beings, we are faced with building relationships daily: at work, church, school, at home with our partners and children. To ensure that we build healthy relationships let us examine some of the things we need to do. I have used the acronym **LATCH** to highlight the important factors. Why **LATCH**?

There are many factors that are vital in relationship building but the ones I will be highlighting are foundational pillars for a functional relationship. The first letter in each word combines to form the word **LATCH**:

LOVE

ACCEPTANCE

TRUST

COMMUNICATION

HONESTY

What is a latch?

- It is used to fasten doors or windows.
- How does, the latch work?
- There are two parts, and one part fits into the other.
- What if the parts do not fit?
- You will not be able to close your windows and doors.

I will describe the latch that is not fitting as malfunctioning.

I believe by this you must be wondering about my trend of thoughts which I will now explain . . .

In any human relationship persons have to be able to get along together to have a healthy relationship. When there are conflicts, just like the malfunctioning latch, these persons will not relate well to each other and so they will have dysfunctional relationships.

Have you ever experienced a dysfunctional relationship? It can be deemed to be 'a mini world war' where some of the things that are likely to happen include verbal abuse, physical abuse, emotional abuse ....
(Include your suggestions in the space provided). However, when Jesus is in the midst of the relationship, He brings peace.

God wants us to love one another, the way He loves us, just as we are:

> "But God demonstrates his own love toward us, in that while we were still sinners, Christ died for us."
>
> ~ *Romans 5:8*

What I am about to say next is going to be a big surprise to many persons who have a perception of love as receiving and not giving. There may be those of you who are quick to highlight that you are not loved because you do not get what you want in a relationship (always wanting to say, 'Thank you' but never wanting to say, 'You are welcome'). Oh yes! There are others who are willing to say, 'Me too' when someone says to you, "I love you" but you are never the first to express love verbally or otherwise.

To the 'receivers' in relationships God is saying that love is giving of the self and that entails sacrifice:

> *"For God so loved the world that He gave His only begotten Son, that whoever believes in Him should not perish but have everlasting life."*
>
> *~ John 3:16*

Let's examine the **LATCH** factors starting with love as demonstrated in I Corinthians 13.

LOVE is the root system that sustains relationships and relationship building. Paul helps us to understand that our perception of love might be centred on being kind but if we are insincere in our motives it is a futile exercise:

> *"And though I bestow all my goods to feed the poor, and though I give my body to be burned, but have not love it profits me nothing."*
>
> *~ 1 Corinthians 13: 3*

So far it is clear that love is not an impression building exercise. So what is love? Let us read each subsequent verse of 1 Corinthians 13 and I will share with you my thoughts:

> *"Love suffers long and is kind; love does not envy; love does not parade itself, is not puffed up."*
>
> *~ 1 Corinthians 13: 4*

Let's do some introspection and if we are envious and like to show off, let us ask Jesus to help us to be humble as He was when He was on earth. Let's examine the next verse:

"Does not behave rudely, does not seek its own, is not provoked, thinks no evil."

~ 1 Corinthians 13: 5

This verse highlights the model character we should demonstrate in love. If you love, as God commands us to do, you should be respectful. In being respectful, you would not be rude to others ('does not behave rudely'), you would not be selfish and so you would respect the rights of other (does not seek its own). You would not allow yourself to be reduced to provocation to belittle yourself ('is not provoked'). If you genuinely love God, you would demonstrate all the characteristics of respect in the sight of God including keeping your thoughts pure.

"Does not rejoice in iniquity, but rejoices in the truth.

~ 1 Corinthians 13: 6

This is interesting. God is reminding us that we should not rejoice if evil befalls anyone. If you are rejoicing, ensure that this is done for what is honest and upright, that is, the truth.

"Bears all things, believes all things, hopes all things, endures all things."

~ 1 Corinthians 13:7

Let's work through this final verse together:
What does it mean when one 'bears all things'? This means, that whatever happens we need to be able to cope. 'Believes all things' – this does not mean that you are gullible by believing

everything that you hear or see from anyone who has a story to tell and who appears convincing. When Jesus speaks of believing what does He mean? Jesus is referring to everything you hear concerning the Word of God. To know the Word of God you will have to read.

'Hopes all things', is encouraging us to operate with expectancy. This means that we are to 'act' as if the things we desire are happening. Let's use some everyday examples as I usually do to demonstrate this:

You have applied for a mortgage on a house that you have fallen in love with. Be honest, do you sit and wait passively? No, not at all! You start looking at paint colour charts to choose the colour for each room in the house, looking around at furniture (I know I would get you all excited!). Please complete the many other ways you demonstrate hope in the space provided..

You have just met the young (or old) lady or man of your dreams. Do not forget that some people find their partners later in life than others. Hope keeps you all excited. You start planning the engagement party from the first time you communicated. You have not gone on a date as yet but you have planned the wedding and the children you will have. For the older folks they might be thinking of how to gain acceptance of the children each partner might have had previously, ...

....

....

(Include other examples in the space provided).

Words of warning! Do not allow yourself to be carried away to the extent that you plan a house warming before the mortgage approval as in the first example.

In the second example, do not send out your engagement or wedding invitations until both parties have mutually agreed to spend their lives together.

Without hope things would be really dull as there would be no anticipation in our lives. Life would be very boring just waiting to see what happens next.

My understanding of the last section of verse 7, 'endures all things', means that regardless of how painful, humiliating, annoying, unfair a situation or your circumstance might be, you live with it without complaining that life is unfair.

David's life is a good example of endurance. Saul and David's son, Absolam tried to kill him yet he endured without complaining. When Absolam was killed David cried and wished he had died instead of his son. That is endurance. Would you have acted like David?

I want to focus on two more verses that will help to cement our understanding of the importance of love:

> *"Love never fails. But whether there are prophecies, they will fail; whether there are tongues, they will cease; whether there is knowledge it will vanish away."*
>
> *~ 1 Corinthians 13: 8*

This verse needs no explanation. The first three words say it all, 'Love never fails'.

Look at your life in retrospect. Have you told anyone or been told by anyone the words, "I love you" and then the relationship ends and there is no longer any communication between yourself and that person? If your answer is yes I hope you know that was not love as love never fails.

The importance of love is reiterated in the final verse:

THE WORD

"And now abide faith, hope, love, these three: but the greatest of these is love."

~ 1 Corinthians 13:13

Using 1 Corinthians 13 as a guide, in the space provided make a list of some of the things you failed at in loving others.

....
....
....

Re-check your list and ensure you have included everything you failed at and then ask God to help you make the necessary changes.

Please include the changes you experienced after receiving God's help below:

....
....
....

After reading 1 Corinthians chapter 13, I have a better understanding of what love entails. I therefore need to apply the characteristics of love highlighted in these passages to my own life wholeheartedly. What about you? Remember the characteristics you need to display include kindness, patience, humility, unselfishness (include others you have learnt from 1 Corinthians 13).

....
....
....

RELATIONSHIP BUILDING

ACCEPTANCE, a key factor in relationship building, is an unconditional acknowledgement of self and others without pretense or excuses. The first thing you have to do is to accept the person as he or she is. Would you wait until your child becomes a doctor, lawyer, scientist, athlete, ………………………….. (include your career choice in the space provided) before you accept him or her? No! You would accept your child as he or she is now, making all the mistakes that are a part of the learning process of life which include even failing sometimes in school. What I am really trying to say is that acceptance should not be conditional; that is, based upon a person's looks, achievement or other factors.

I need some feedback from partners in relationships.

Husbands, wives, boyfriends, girlfriends, potential partners, do you wait until your partner is successful financially or has completed the diet, exercise and plastic surgery to look good? I will remind you, however, that you could become disillusioned if the money 'goes' or the person becomes less attractive with the passage of time. Remember even with plastic surgery signs of aging will still be visible because aging is a natural part of God's creation. It is very important to learn to accept yourself and others as you all are: fat, slim, rich, poor, articulate, inarticulate and the list is endless . . . .

Finally, we need to remember that when we accept ourselves and others we are allowed to make changes in our own lives or suggestions to others that are deemed beneficial. Do not change to please others but make changes that are necessary as part of your growth process. Do not go on a fad diet because people want you to be slim as it is fashionable. Diet if you believe there are health benefits to be derived.

TRUST is another important factor in building relationships. Trust is built up over time when there is honest communication. When one person realizes that the other is always honest then it is easier to believe or accept as true what is said or done. This results in complete loyalty so that one believes that other individual when others doubt the authenticity of his or her action or statement.

Let me illustrate the importance of trust in a relationship:

- A parent (mother or father) has a child who is very rebellious; but that child has never taken money without asking for it, despite that money being conspicuously placed in the house.

- Trust has been built in the relationship between parent and child as a result of this.

- The parent knows that his or her child is honest. At school, the child is accused of stealing money from another student's school bag.

- This parent would passionately defend the integrity of his or her child because of their existing relationship. There is honest communication and over time trust has been built up.

- This parent, knowing the integrity of his or her child, would be confident that in time the guilty person would be identified so that his or her child would be exonerated.

COMMUNICATION is the way we relate to each other. We should be able to talk to each other about anything which includes our feelings, aspirations, spirituality, failures and weaknesses. When we communicate, it enables us to learn from each other thereby providing opportunities for growth in the different facets of our lives, including our spiritual growth. Many persons are afraid to express themselves about their lack of understanding of spiritual and other matters. I encourage you to read and to challenge each other with questions that arise from your own personal reading exercises.

In communicating, we sometimes find it difficult in complimenting each other for our positive attributes. Instead, we tend to remain silent. On the other hand, when someone does something wrong, it is so easy to criticize and condemn that person (don't worry you are not alone I am also guilty). Communication dictates that we should not conceal anything and we should also be generous with our compliments.

A reminder to males and females who enjoy flattering persons in order to boost their egos . . . Please stop doing that now! We need to give genuine compliments to each other so do not mislead someone into believing that what you are saying about them is sincere when you know it is not. How do you think that person will feel when it is revealed that you said the things you did for your own selfish motives? It would mean, 'bye-bye relationship'. In addition, we would have displeased God by not communicating honestly with each other:

"And just as you want men to do to you, you also do to them likewise."

~ Luke 6:31

Communicate with each other in the way you would want them to relate to you. I know how easy it is to criticize and condemn others for the wrongs they have done. No one wants you to pat the person on the back for their acts of wrong doing.

However, you should be sensitive to the person's feelings and communicate in love. In this way persons will maintain their sense of dignity and self worth as human beings whilst learning to take corrective actions where appropriate.

We need to remember that we all have strengths and weaknesses and we all enjoy praise and hate corrections. Let us look at ourselves first by accepting our own strengths and weaknesses in order to appreciate and accept other as we communicate.

We should recognize that we have a Christian responsibility to help each other to identify as well as to improve in areas of weaknesses. I know it is not an easy assignment to highlight areas of weaknesses to each other as we fear how the other person will react. On the other hand, when our roles are reversed and we are the ones being corrected, our pride makes it very difficult to acknowledge this and be willing to learn and grow in order to improve in these areas.

Since God expects us to be caring human beings, let us help each other using the subtle lesson Jesus uses to reprimand us:

> *'And why do you look at the speck in your brother's eye, but do not consider the plank in your own eye? "Or how can you say to your brother, 'Let me remove the speck from your eye'; and look, a plank is in your own eye?" Hypocrite! First remove the plank from your own eye, and then you will see clearly to remove the speck from your brother's eye.'*
>
> *~ Matthew 7: 3–5*

Jesus used two words to highlight our hypocrisy, plank and speck. Who has the plank in their eyes? The ones who are eager to condemn others, those of us who believe we are so p-e-r-f-e-c-t and have no sin. However, we are not perfect and we need

Jesus to guide and to correct us. Jesus reminds the so called perfect ones that their imperfection is so conspicuous that it is visible to the entire world by using the analogy of a plank! What is a plank? According to *The Little Oxford Dictionary and Thesaurus*, it is a long flat piece of timber. Do you get the point? The whole world is seeing your weakness. It is long and is obvious to the world. In other words, your weaknesses are greater than the other person's, which Jesus refers to as a speck. Yet despite your log or your glaring weakness you want to criticize or magnify some trivial fault in the other person's life. That is hypocrisy for we are not communicating as Jesus wants us to do.

I hope based on what Jesus has highlighted in the passage above that we should all agree that we ought to consider our own weaknesses and bear these in mind so that we can be sensitive to the feelings of others as we highlight and suggest recommendations for their weaknesses.

Please remember that communication is not only verbal but includes our body language and facial expressions (unspoken words) which also impact our relationships with each other.

Communicate and interact with sensitivity as you build healthy relationships.

HONESTY is an important factor in relationship building and an important quality in your character. The word character refers to those consistent qualities that make you who you are. These qualities will remain the same wherever you are and whomever you are with. In other words, you are genuine and so your words can be relied on and one does not have to question your integrity. In being honest, one's actions and words must be consistent over time. If you do not like something you should not pretend in order to please the other person.

If you are aware of your own weaknesses such as anger and impatience you find it much easier to speak out about these than to conceal them. On the other hand, the dishonest person is more likely to mislead others about weaknesses in their lives. However, when the truth is revealed, it becomes more difficult thereafter to trust that person as there will always be the unanswered question: 'What else is being concealed?' That person would have now assumed the role of an actor and that is unhealthy for relationships.

For persons who are dishonest, I offer some words of advice if your performance in real life in your relationship is discovered as acting, you could lose that potential relationship or that relationship that you really treasured. Acting or dishonesty stifles relationships.

In relationships, many persons have a perception of what the other partner expects. These persons believe that in order to be loved they have to meet those expectations and so they will be pretentious in order to achieve their objectives.

Included in this category are persons who want to be regarded as affluent when in reality they are not. So, they might drive an expensive car and live in an expensive apartment that is really unaffordable but they do so in order to seek validation.

However, these persons cannot be accused of lying with words (you will not hear them saying , 'I am rich') but their lifestyle is a misrepresentation of who they really are. They have not accepted themselves and so they need an outward show to cover the reality of their lives as they are concerned about their reputation. Reputation is defined by *The Little Oxford Dictionary and Thesaurus* as what is generally believed about a person or thing. Please note the use of the word generally, which connotes that a certain amount of stereotyping takes place.

You get my drift, right? In stereotyping, your house, your car and clothes are all status symbols used to conceal your true identity in order to impress or deceive others.

Reputation then, which is pleasing the world by meeting the criteria set, is more important to these persons than a consistent demonstration of their character (which is who they really are at all times regardless of where they are or who they are with).

Friends, the losses are great when you lie in your relationships whether at school with your teachers or peers, at work with your co-workers, boss or at home with your partner and children.

Do you really want to live your life being dishonest? Do you want to be caught in your own trap and see that relationship crumble before your eyes because of lying? Think twice!! Jesus reminds us of the importance of being honest:

> *Behold You desire truth in the inward parts, and in the hidden part You will make me to know wisdom.*
>
> ~ Psalm 51:6

Read the first part of the verse aloud:

Behold You desire truth in the inward parts.

What message are those words sending to you? Do your examination and indicate your understanding of the message below:

....

THE WORD

Now reflect on your past and on those times you might have been dishonest in your relationship in order to win the approval of your partner, children, co-workers or other persons.

God wants us to be honest in our very thoughts. Always remember that only God knows our thoughts so do not allow anyone to trick you into thinking otherwise. If we practise what God expects of us in an effort to be obedient to Him we will learn to accept ourselves. In addition, we will be willing to be honest in self disclosure with others without worrying about the consequences when the truth is revealed about us. Here are my words of advice to all of us: where we are guilty of lying let us stop and start speaking the truth at all times as God wants us to do.

There are some persons, however, who are so concerned about not hurting the feelings of others that they would rather lie than be honest. Is that the right thing to do? God wants us in these situations as well to be honest with each other so that we are able to learn and grow in the process. I have good news for all those persons who are very sensitive and get easily offended when faced with the truth. Your friends have been so afraid to be honest with you that they have stifled your growth process. I am here to help you to grow and build your character. Here are some words of advice:

Accept the truth spoken in love so that you can make the necessary changes in your life. Persons will then be able to tell you the truth without an explosion (you getting angry), flood waters (your tears) or an internal turmoil (your thoughts and feelings going awry). I know that with regard to your hurt feelings your comments might include some of the following:

- You do not understand, no one has ever hurt your feelings
- I have been very sensitive from childhood
- My mother did this . . . . My father did that
- My sister is unkind
- My friends laugh at me
- My husband is a verbal abuser
- Other reasons that you might want to include in the space provided ....

Life is about growth. You have to allow yourself to grow spiritually, intellectually, emotionally or in other facets of your life.

Accept life's experiences whatever they may be, whether it is a failure at something or some one's honest opinion, as an opportunity to make an assessment and take corrective actions. Your bad experiences with hurt feelings are really sad but it's time to face life honestly now. Let us live our lives honestly, the way Jesus taught us. Please remember, honesty frees us and dishonesty as well as sensitivity entraps us.

Are you practising LATCH in your relationship with others? If you are, please continue to; if not, start right now. We have worked on ways to improve our human relationships but the question is, How does the LATCH principle work in our relationship with God?

The principle of relationship building with Jesus is similar to building relationships with each other:

L OVE – Jesus loves us and gave his life sacrificially so we will be able to benefit from his love here on earth as well as eternally.

THE WORD

ACCEPTANCE – Jesus accepts us as we are. He knows our thoughts, what we will do and so we do not have to impress Him. Peter is a good example of an impressionist. The difference is, we do not know the person's thoughts but Jesus does. Let's look at the conversation that Jesus had with His disciples after the Passover:

> *Then Jesus said to them, "All of you will be made to stumble because of Me this night, for it is written: I will strike the Shepherd, and the sheep of the flock will be scattered."*
>
> *~ Matthew 26:31*

Listen now to the impressionist, Peter:

> *Peter answered and said to Him, 'Even if all are made to stumble because of You, I will never be made to stumble."*
>
> *~ Matthew 26:33*

The world has a fair number of persons like Peter both males and females.

How many of us have been impressionists at work? "I want to grow with this organization and I have no plans to leave this place." (Do we really mean it or do we say so because we want to get the job?)

How many of us have been impressionists in our relationships? "I will always love you regardless of the nature of the conflict between us" (before any serious conflict occurs we disappear without any forwarding address).

Remember I said earlier that God accepts us as we are despite all the things He knows about us. Jesus demonstrated this with Peter:

RELATIONSHIP BUILDING

Jesus said to him, "Assuredly, I say to you that this night, before the rooster crows you will deny me three times."

~ Matthew 26:34

If I were in Peter's position I would do some serious soul searching before saying anything else that I would not be able to live up to. Imagine Jesus knows everything about us and He does not lie so it means that Peter's denial will happen as Jesus said. Peter, however, continued his impression building:

Peter said to Him, "Even if I have to die with You, I will not deny you!" And so said all the disciples.

~ Matthew 26:35

We all know that as Jesus had stated Peter ended up denying Him, but Peter regretted it after:

Then he began to curse and swear, saying, "I do not know the Man!" Immediately a rooster crowed. And Peter remembered the word of Jesus who had said to him,

"Before the rooster crows, you will deny Me three times." So he went out and wept bitterly.

~ Matthew 26: 74-75

We are all humans and in one way or another we are like Peter from time to time. It is important to remember at all times that we cannot fool God and it is not right to impress the people in the world as they cannot save our souls. Indeed, your actions might be impressive to the world as you are in church every Sunday and you sing on the choir and give generously.

If your motive is wrong, God is not pleased and so everything you do will be leading you away from eternity.

THE WORD

I will now share with you what God said to Samuel about Eliab, David's brother, to substantiate my point that God looks at the heart and not at the things that impress us as human beings:

But the Lord said to Samuel, "Do not look at his appearance or at his physical stature, because I have refused him. For the Lord does not see as man sees; for man looks at the outward appearance, but the Lord looks at the heart."

~ 1 Samuel 16:7

TRUST in our relationship with God enables us to be confident that He will take care of us despite our circumstance. Peter demonstrated this in Matthew chapter 14 in the midst of the storm when the other disciples, on seeing Jesus, were convinced that he was a ghost. Peter, however trusted Jesus and he knew that if it was really Jesus and not a ghost he would be able to walk on water (in a raging storm!) and not drown. Before we look at the verses relating to Peter let me reiterate – you trust Jesus when you allow yourself to believe and grow in your relationship with Him through your experiences over time.

Let's read the passage together now:

And when the disciples saw Him walking on the sea, they were troubled, saying, "It is a ghost!" And they cried out for fear. But immediately Jesus spoke to them saying, "Be of good cheer! It is I do not be afraid." And Peter answered Him and said, "Lord, if it is You, command me to come to You on the water." So He said, "Come." And when Peter had come down out of the boat, he walked on the water to go to Jesus.

~ Matthew 14: 26-29

I love this passage with Peter walking on water as it demonstrates our human weaknesses as we face challenges (see additional references to Peter walking on water in chapter 6). We claim to trust God but when the circumstances become really difficult we begin to doubt.

Trust always triumphs in our moments of doubt and fear. If you genuinely trust God, even in your darkest moment of despair you can rise up to say the most important words, 'Lord save me' to transform your life (or save it literally) like Peter. When you do, you are guaranteed the outstretched hands of Jesus to save you:

> *And immediately Jesus stretched out His hand and caught him, and said to him, "O you of little faith, why did you doubt?"*
>
> *~ Matthew 14:31*

Trust God and you will always be happy in your relationship with Him.

COMMUNICATION in our relationship with God allows us to express respectfully to God our feelings, pain, doubts, desires and our gratitude. God reveals His plan and purpose for our lives as we communicate with Him and express our desire to do His will.

In communicating with us, God gives us His commandments as well as the consequences when we are disobedient. Although God is powerful, He is not a dictator as He has given us a free will to make our choices bearing in mind the consequences. God dialogues with us and so when we look at Genesis chapter 3: 8–13, we see where God communicated with Adam and Eve regarding their disobedient act.

THE WORD

God invites us through His Word to dialogue or reason with Him in our relationship because he loves us and wants the best for us (Isaiah 1: 18-20)

Remember in our earthly communication we allow one person to speak whilst we listen and we should apply this principle to listen to God as He speaks to us through His ministers, teachers, our neighbours, partners, friends, children and others. Let us demonstrate the respect towards God that Eli taught Samuel:

> *Therefore Eli said to Samuel ,"Go lie down; and it shall be, if He calls you, that you must say, "Speak, Lord, for your servant hears." So Samuel went and lay down in his place. Now the Lord came and stood and called as at other times, "Samuel! Samuel!" and Samuel answered, "Speak, for your servant hears."*
>
> *~1 Samuel 3: 9-10*

Communicate with God by reading His Word, and learn more about Him through the many bible characters highlighted. In addition, pray, give thanks and ask for God's guidance in your lives.

HONESTY is inevitable if you are in a relationship with God. However, God knows that as human beings we would rather be dishonest than admit our acts of wrong doing and so He provides an opportunity for us to make amends when we do wrong:

> *If we confess our sins, He is faithful and just to forgive us our sins and to cleanse us from all unrighteousness.*
>
> *~1 John 1:9*

RELATIONSHIP BUILDING

LATCH your relationship with God and with others and enjoy this life on earth and look forward to enjoying eternity. Remember your latch might malfunction sometimes but examine what went wrong and take corrective actions.

God Bless you.

– 5 –

Faith

In your relationship with Jesus I am confident that you share your testimony when you get the things you desire. Oh! It is so easy to stand up and tell the world how God is faithful and He is doing great things in your life.

Let's say two weeks later you are made redundant and you attend church after your job loss and your pastor asks for a testimony. Be honest with me now, would God still be the miracle working God that you spoke of at times when all your desires were met, or would you now sit silently as you no longer have a job to boast about?

Come on . . . We have to learn that God is not there waiting to give us all the things that we want when we want them. God has a plan and a purpose and sometimes He uses our disappointments to build our character and our faith in Him. We as human beings face crisis situations from time to time where God appears to be silent and He is not giving us the things we desire. What do we do? If we stop trusting God then we are no longer loyal, obedient or have faith. Once our faith building experience stops, we suddenly wake up to a place of unbelief. Unless, of course, we get what we want from God, right?

We spend our time asking God questions and telling God the reasons we no longer believe. God does not pamper us to our detriment so do not think you can persuade God to do anything that prevents Him from getting the glory. Wake up! Right now, you might try the emotional act with your friends and partner and it works, but God knows your heart and what is best for you so humble yourself and let His will be done.

God does not pretend as we do. He is not human and He never lies. If you pray and do not get the response you desire, remember that God's timing is not like yours and that He has a better plan.

We need to change our perspective and worship and adore God for who He is and not for what He gives to us. When we have faith in our Heavenly Father, our Creator, then we will appreciate the fact that He is working as God who is omnipotent, omniscient and not as humans who focus on materialism. As long as we keep our eyes on God, we will not murmur or complain over material things like the Israelites going through the wilderness. God is not pleased with us when we murmur. Verify this with the biblical record of how God dealt with the Israelites (Numbers 11: 1).

The biblical example of Moses' faith building experience with God provides an opportunity for us to learn from him and apply it in our lives. Please read Exodus chapters 3 and 4 for the complete story.

In summary, at the time God called Moses to the leadership position he did not have a relationship with God. In the initial stage Moses doubted God and argued constantly:

THE WORD

But Moses said to God, 'Who am I that I should go to Pharaoh and that I should bring the children of Israel out of Egypt.

~ Exodus 3:11

Then Moses said to God, "Indeed, when I come to the children of Israel and say to them, 'The God of your Fathers has sent me to you,' and they say to me, 'What is His name?' what shall I say to them?"

~ Exodus 3:13

God was patient with Moses as He understood that his faith was weak and would only be strengthened through his experiences with Him and so God responded accordingly:

"And God said to Moses, 'I AM WHO I AM.' And He said, 'Thus you shall say to the children of Israel, 'I AM has sent me to you." Moreover God said to Moses, 'Thus you shall say to the children of Israel: 'The Lord God of your Fathers, the God of Abraham, the God of Isaac, and the God of Jacob, has sent me to you. This is My name forever, and this is My memorial to all generations.'

~ Exodus 3: 14–15

I am sure that like me you believe that after God provided Moses with the name he asked for he would have been merrily on his way to tell the children of Israel about his encounter with God. Oh! No! Moses still lacked faith. Listen to his next question:

Then Moses answered and said, "But suppose they will not believe me or listen to my voice; suppose they say, 'The Lord has not appeared to you."

~ Exodus 4:1

What I find very fascinating is when Moses fled from his rod which became a serpent when God instructed him to cast the rod to the ground:

> *"So the Lord said to him, "What is that in your hand?" He said, "A rod." And He said, "Cast it on the ground." So he cast it on the ground, and it became a serpent; and Moses fled from it."*
>
> *~ Exodus 4: 2–3*

Moses' faith was still in the developmental stage and he was not yet exposed to the miracle working power of God. This meant that as far as he was concerned if that serpent bit him it would be fatal. Moses was not prepared to take that chance as God's miraculous power in transforming a rod to a snake took him off guard. I am sure, however, that mentally it was a great faith-building lesson for him and I must confess my deduction is based on what Moses did next:

> *Then the Lord said to Moses, "Reach out your hand and take it by the tail" (and he reached out his hand and caught it, and it became a rod in his hand).*
>
> *~ Exodus 4:4*

Moses was now able to take that serpent by the tail not running away this time but believing in the power of God that was demonstrated to him through God's signs using his rod. He had come to the place where he believed and had faith in God. He followed God's instruction to take that serpent by the tail without asking God, 'Why'? Moses did not know that God was going to turn the snake back into his rod. However, he learnt through that experience that God was demonstrating His power to him and he was learning to have faith in God.

In order for your faith to grow it has to be challenged. This means that as you are exposed to greater trials you are likely to slip back into periods of doubt until your faith grows. This happens as you reflect on your previous experiences with God or are reminded about His awesome power as you share with others.

Let us now examine what happened to Moses after that awesome experience with the rod turning into a snake and then the snake being turned back into a rod. Moses went through another period where his faith wavered. He did not believe that he could manage that mammoth task of leading the children of Israel despite the reassurance from God. Moses came up with an excuse that he hoped God would accept:

> *Then Moses said to the Lord, "O my lord, I am not eloquent, neither before or since You have spoken to Your servant, but I am slow of speech and slow of tongue."*
>
> *~ Exodus 4:10*

Moses tried to be convincing about his lack of eloquence by highlighting to God that his speech disability was an existing problem. In my own words he was saying, 'I am not using my lack of eloquence as an excuse; it is a genuine problem that I have always had.' Of course we know that God has the power to help Moses and is willing to help us today with areas of weaknesses in our lives once we trust Him.

Please read the remainder of Exodus chapter 4 to learn more about weaknesses demonstrated by Moses as he battled with building his faith. Like Moses, we too will have times when we doubt God but all we need to do is to communicate our doubts and fears to God so that He can help us as we climb the ladder of faith successfully.

Similarly, the book of Daniel also provides us with examples of persons who demonstrated great faith in God during trying circumstances. In Daniel chapter 3, we look at three men who demonstrated faith in God in circumstances that I know I would have failed in. What about you?

Shadrach, Meshach and Abed-Nego refused to worship Nebuchadnezzar's image of gold and were told that they would be cast into the fiery furnace.

These three men demonstrated their faith in God by their response to Nebuchadnezzar, king of Babylon:

> *"If that is the case, our God who we serve is able to deliver us from the burning fiery furnace, and He will deliver us from your hand O king. But if not, let it be known to you, O king, that we do not serve your gods, nor will we worship the gold image which you have set up."*
>
> *~ Daniel 3: 17-18*

Read Daniel 3: 22-26. In those verses you will see God's power demonstrated through the faithfulness of these three men. The furnace was extremely hot and the men who cast them in the furnace died. These three men were not alone as God was with them in the fiery furnace and so they came out alive and unharmed.

Wow! Wow! That's awesome!! God is good. Would you be able to exercise that level of faith in God? Think about it.

The level of faith of these three men helped Nebuchadnezzar to believe in our God (Daniel 3: 24-30)

We too, like these three men, can bring glory to God when we demonstrate our faith in God so others are able to see in times of our trial.

In order to grow healthily your 'faith plant' needs to be

fertilized by reading your Bible, praying, and thanking God for all the things He has done for you including His plan of salvation. You should always remember that the enemy wants you to doubt God so when you fertilize your faith, you defeat him.

Without strong faith in God, it will be difficult to cope in these challenging times.

Faith in God should not waver when God takes longer than we anticipate in answering our prayers. What we should do is to use the time to reflect on God's goodness while we wait.

God reminds us in His Word that it is impossible to please Him without faith. This should convince us of the importance of faith in our lives. Faith however cannot succeed alongside its 'enemy'.

Faith's 'enemy' is doubt which enjoys being a companion on every journey if it is entertained. You therefore need to learn how to ignore this 'enemy' on your faith journey or risk not receiving your miracles or achieving your goals. It is important to understand that not all our desires fail to come to fruition because of doubt and so by a process of identification and elimination other reason(s) can be discovered.

Let us now examine some possible reasons based on our experiences:

- Our desires are not in accordance with God's will for our lives.

- We become impatient and give up.

- We ask but are not prepared to seek and knock. In other words, we want everything to happen with minimal effort on our part.

- Include your reasons in the space provided

....
....
....

In many instances, however, the one reason that prevents many of us from succeeding in the realm of faith is, doubt. Where there is doubt, dreams and desires remain unconquered.

- If your faith is small you can remove mountains
- If your doubt is small it chokes your faith and makes the mountain you want to remove impossible.
- To succeed by faith you need to remove every element of doubt.

Let us read what Jesus told His disciples as they marveled at how quickly the fig tree withered at His command. Their response attested to the negative impact of doubt:

And when the disciples saw it, they marveled saying, "How did the fig tree wither away so soon? So Jesus answered and said to them, "Assuredly, I say to you, if you have faith and do not doubt, you will not only do what was done to the fig tree, but also if you say to this mountain, 'Be removed and be cast into the sea it will be done."

~ Matthew 21: 20-21

Jesus is reminding us that our faith should not be mingled with doubt if we want to achieve our desires. Faith then is complete trust in God regardless of our circumstances. In other words, we remain faithful to God for who He is and not only for what we can get from Him materially. What is doubt? I have used my favourite approach, an acronym, to help you to understand:

DEBARRING

OPPORTUNITIES

UNSEEN

BY MY

THOUGHTS

Doubt begins in the mind. Once you start thinking negatively this thought pattern translates into your behaviour. These negative thoughts can arise as a result of a number of factors including:

- Low self esteem – When you believe that you cannot achieve certain things as you see yourself as unworthy. You are made in the image of God and are deserving of the best things in life. You have to believe this as no one else can convince you. Allow low self esteem to fade away and replace it with high self esteem. Be confident about who you are and what you can achieve.

- Fear of failure – This may be attributed to a past experience where you believed you would have succeeded but failed. Take some time to analyse your past failure and learn from it by asking and answering the following questions:

- Was there something that I should have done and did not do?

- Did I listen to the negative assessment of my abilities by others?

- Did I give up too quickly?
- Did I fail because I doubted my abilities?

Doubt should not be entertained because of its destructive force but when it exists the question is:

- How do I eliminate doubt from my thoughts?
- Accept that you are a child of God, made in His image and that God wants you to prosper.

Remember God expects us to have faith but He also expects us to work at whatever it is we need to achieve:

"Thus also faith by itself, if it does not have works, is dead."

~ James 2:17

You cannot hold on to your faith only and expect to achieve, for God wants you to work as you demonstrate faith.

I will illustrate the point. You have lost your job as a result of a redundancy exercise. You have been praying to God to provide another and you are confident that you have the faith that God will provide this job for you.

To ensure that your faith is equally matched by your effort the following would be expected:

- Sending out applications
- Attending interviews
- Make follow up calls for interviews done to see if you have been selected for the position. If you have not been selected do not throw up your hands in despair. Instead, repeat the process by sending out more applications and making your

follow up calls. Do not forget that God in His Word makes it explicit that we are to ask, seek and knock. If your qualification needs upgrading, do so.

You are now more cognizant of factors that are deterrent to faith building including the 'enemy' doubt, and how to overcome these.

All you need to do now is to have faith in God and use His Word to remind you of its importance in your life:

But without faith it is impossible to please Him, for he who comes to God must believe that He is and that He is a rewarder of those who diligently seek Him.

~ Hebrews 11:6

– 6 –

Overcoming Challenges

An individual's perception of his or her situation will eventually determine how he or she copes when faced with challenges. Do you agree?

Regardless of your view, the reality is that challenges are a part of life and so we all face them daily whether we are prepared for them or not.

Exciting news! When we know Jesus, we are assured that God is alive and is helping us to overcome our challenges. Read on if you doubt me:

> *"You are of God, little children and have overcome them, because He who is in you is greater than he who is in the world."*
>
> *~1 John 4:4*

God reassures us that we are not alone and all we need to do is to ask for His help when we face challenges. In the Bible there are a number of occasions where Bible characters faced numerous challenges and God guided them through all of these. These Bible characters were successful in overcoming the challenges they faced because they believed in and had a relationship with God and were faithful (I am sure you will now endorse the importance of the previous chapters on believing, relationship building and faith).

It is important to note that if you ask for God's guidance but choose to act in a manner that is conflicting with God's standard by acting dishonestly or illegally, do not blame God when your plan fails:

> *Unless the Lord builds the house, they labor in vain who build it; Unless the Lord guards the city, the watchman stays awake in vain.*
>
> *~ Psalm 127:1*

In other words, whatever you do without applying God's guidelines, you will ultimately fail. You might succeed for a while and doubt that you need God's guidance but I suggest that you think seriously about including God in your plans.

When you ask God for his help, prepare to be patient as God's timing and yours will not be the same. David knew how impatient we are and so he emphasized the importance of waiting on God in Psalm 27. Let us read together:

> *Wait on the Lord; be of good courage, and he shall strengthen your heart; Wait I say on the Lord.*
>
> *~ Psalm 27:14.*

As you read the verse what became conspicuous to you?

Right! In one verse David emphasized wait, twice. I am sure David has helped you to understand the importance of waiting.

Now that we understand that waiting is a prerequisite in receiving God's help, let us examine in greater detail more on overcoming challenges. What did Jesus have to say about challenges?

OVERCOMING CHALLENGES

In John 16: 33 Jesus reminds his disciples that they will face challenges or tribulations:

"These things I have spoken to you, that in Me you may have peace. In the world you will have tribulation; but be of good cheer, I have overcome the world."

~ John 16:33

Jesus told his disciples to be cheerful about trials or challenges. Jesus has the authority to do so as whilst on earth he faced and overcame temptations and conquered death to give us the opportunity to receive eternal life. Jesus knows our weaknesses but he encourages us to cast our cares on Him:

"Casting all your care upon Him for He cares for you"

~ 1 Peter 5:7

When we trust Jesus we are able to rejoice as we know we can overcome our challenges as Jesus is in control. I know, it is easier said than done especially with doubt being our weakest link in trusting God. Remember, doubting is not unique to some persons; instead, it is common to all of us. Let us look at how Peter's life demonstrated this.

Peter, one of Jesus' disciples was human like us and had his greatest faith experience mingled with doubt as we do too sometimes (think about it . . .).

Many of us today face challenges that make it easy for us to identify with Peter's experience of walking on water.

Today your challenges might not be on a ship which is tossing on the ocean in a storm. Your problem could be financial or relational. Help me as I try to identify some of your specific problems. Financial problems could include:

inadequate salary, job loss, mortgage foreclosure, credit card indebtedness and..
(include others in the space provided).

Relational issues or problems could include: rebellious children, an unfaithful partner, an inconsiderate coworker, an unkind boss. In addition to financial and relational challenges there are other categories you might want to include here

....

....

....

Close your eyes and imagine that you are on the ship with the disciples that night . . . Do you realize how dark it is? Can you hear the sound of the waves swishing? . . . The boat is like a roller coaster. You are wet and cold . . . brrrr . . . Water is dripping all over your face . . . . Your eyes are itching from the salt. That is how boisterous the waves were.

You have visualized yourself being eaten by sharks a thousand times. Oh my gosh and now!! A ghost walking on water! What's next? Dying from fear of the ghost, drowning or both?

Thank God for Peter who was not prepared to roll over and die. Instead, he wanted confirmation that it was Jesus as he knew that they would all be safe with Jesus in control.

The disciples were terrified of the storm as we are today when we face challenges in our lives. Like the disciples, there are many times when in the midst of our crisis Jesus provides a solution, but sometimes we cannot see the solution as we have already perceived a greater problem (your ghost walking on the water). Imagine, Jesus was walking on water to offer help to His disciples in the storm yet they saw reasons to fear:

OVERCOMING CHALLENGES

And when the disciples saw Him walking on the sea, they were troubled, saying, "It is a ghost!" And they cried out for fear.

~ Matthew 14:26

When you have a relationship with Jesus, there are things about Him that you know are consistent: He never lies or fails. He is a miracle worker and He always provides words of comfort.

But immediately Jesus spoke to them saying, "Be of good cheer! It is I do not be afraid."

~ Matthew 14:27

Peter heard the familiar voice and the reassuring words of Jesus and He was ready and willing to demonstrate bravery in that storm. Peter knew that once it was Jesus walking on the water He would be safe and so all he needed was confirmation before stepping out of that boat.

Believing, relationship building and faith are all vital in Peter's experience with Jesus. He had enough faith to know that once Jesus said, "Come" he knew unequivocally that it was Jesus (Matthew 14: 28-29). No human being could invite another to walk on water and remain afloat. They would both drown.

Friends, I must use this opportunity to reiterate the importance of believing, relationship building and faith in Jesus as you can see that those are the key ingredients in overcoming challenges.

I am sure you will all agree with me that the storm symbolizes the challenges we all face in our individual circumstances. Oftentimes we feel overwhelmed by them. However, if we keep our eyes on Jesus, He keeps these challenges under control for us so that we are able to cope (walk on water).

Have you ever heard persons moaning and groaning about their financial difficulties? I also imagine you raising your hand acknowledging that you too find yourself complaining about your financial difficulties. What is usually amazing, however, is to hear these moaners and groaners admit that by the grace of God they are able to survive (raise your hand again). Survival means that these persons are walking on water whether or not they realize it. In other words, Jesus has their financial crises under control (and yours too).

Now let us get back to the scene with Peter walking on the water when the winds became boisterous and he was afraid. We know that to step out of the boat to walk on water is demonstrating faith. I am going to be honest as I have said before I cannot swim and my faith is not that strong. I believe I would be like the other disciples and remain in the boat (if you are like me, admit it).

Peter is human. Although he had faith, he was overwhelmed by his circumstances, the boisterous winds.

Let us translate Peter's action in our own lives today to see if our reaction would be any different. I will use an everyday example:

- Your house needs to be repaired and you trusted God and He provided for you so you were able to do the repairs. Unfortunately your car needs repairing and in addition you have faltered on your car payments. The loan institution is planning to seize your car for the arrears. The car is the sole means of transportation for the family for work, school, church, recreation and other uses.

OVERCOMING CHALLENGES

The boisterous waves (your challenges) are now coming at you like they did with Peter. You are afraid. You are thinking the worst; you are going to lose the car (your ghost).

When fear steps in faith steps out. When faith goes, your eyes are no longer on Jesus and you begin to sink like Peter.

At times like these, some persons start wallowing in self pity. They turn off their phones, inform their office that they are sick, stop going to church and ....
....
(include some of the things you do in the space provided). All these things are signs that you are sinking like Peter.

Remember in those times that God is there with outstretched arms, so just cry out to Him honestly like Peter:

> *But when he saw that the wind was boisterous he was afraid, and beginning to sink he cried out saying, "Lord save me!"*
>
> *~ Matthew 14:30*

Jesus with outstretched arms will help to get you out of your financial or other rut. Remember at all times to call on Jesus as there is no charge attached. All incoming calls to Jesus are free and are guaranteed a response. You will not get a voice mail message to call back later. The fact that you are able to present your case directly to Jesus means that you can be confident that He will provide a solution based on what He knows is best for you. His response might not come as quickly as you desire but when it comes it is perfectly timed to meet your needs.

The boisterous winds that came at Peter represent additional challenges that are coming at you today when you feel that your existing challenges are under control. However, your faith in God will see you through all challenges.

THE WORD

Jesus' words to Peter that his lack of faith had put him in that position to fear and to sink is also a reminder to us today as we face our challenges:

> "O you of little faith, why did you doubt?"
>
> ~ *Matthew 14:31*

Here is the real test for you today when you face challenges:

- Do you believe in Jesus?
- Do you have a relationship with Jesus?
- Do you have faith in Jesus to make a request like Peter did? ("Lord, if it is You, command me to come to You on the water.")

Using Peter's experience with walking on water let us review what we have learnt to help us in overcoming our challenges:

We have to *believe* in Jesus (accept that Jesus' power is real).

A *relationship* with Jesus is vital (getting to know Jesus on a personal level through our experiences).

Faith in Jesus sustains us as we face challenges. All of us are endowed with a measure of faith given by God. As we exercise our faith it grows stronger. However, even If we do not use it we do not lose it. All that happens is that our faith becomes dormant and so it appears as if we are lacking in faith. In many instances, we hear people say, 'I do not have any faith.' They are wrong. All that has happened is that they have failed to exercise their measure of faith:

> *For I say, "through the grace given to me, to everyone who is among you, not to think of himself more highly than he ought to think, but to think*

soberly, as God has dealt to each one a measure of faith."

~ Romans 12:3

God has provided *resources* to help us as we go through our challenges but sometimes we are too busy being afraid to even stop to ask ourselves, 'What do I have that can help me cope with these challenges?' Peter relied on his spiritual resources.

Do you believe that each one of you is endowed by God with resources that will enable you to overcome your challenges?

Let us now look in greater details at the different types of resources available to us:

Spiritual Resources include the faith God has endowed us with, prayer and fasting. Our spiritual resources can help us to recognize the power of God when we call on Him:

'Call to Me, and I will answer you, and show you great and mighty things, which you do not know.'

~ Jeremiah 33:3

In addition it helps us become aware that we are not alone:

". . . I will never leave you nor forsake you"

~ Hebrews 13:5

Tangible Resources include our homes, motor vehicles
....
(include your tangible resources in the space provided).

Your tangible resources could be used as collateral for loans to aid you during your challenging period. However, you should be careful not to over extend your resources and thereby avoid having to sell some of your assets if you are unable to meet your payments.

Please seek financial advice from someone trustworthy before making any decision to use your tangible resources as collateral.

Financial Resources include our income, loan institutions, families and friends that are financially successful that are willing to help us in our times of need ....(include other financial resources in the space provided). Financial resources will provide the cash needed in times of challenge.

Human Resources include our families and friends who provide us with moral and spiritual support and persons with expertise who provide answers to our questions, guide us and make meaningful recommendations. There are some persons who perform the role of moral, spiritual as well as financial supporters and we need to thank God specifically for each role provided by such persons.

Caution. Please ensure that persons who offer assistance are not those who expect you do things displeasing in the sight of God by accepting financial assistance derived from dishonest and illegal means...(include other ways that would be displeasing to God).

Intellectual Resources include the ability to deliberate business ideas or designs that can generate income that will help in times of financial need. The ability to articulate is another gift from God that we sometimes take for granted. This gift has helped many persons to prevent foreclosure, receive rescheduling of debts and lengthened loan periods for repayment.

Please use your gifts.. ....

(include your gifts in the space provided) to help you positively, not to bemoan your state of affairs.

I know economists, accountants and human resource personnel might not agree with my definition of the various types of resources. However, these types are used to help my readers identify the resources available to them in the context of overcoming challenges.

Although the various categories of resources are detailed above we do not necessarily use all of the resources in each category. The important thing when faced with challenges is to act with what we can use based on our circumstance.

Let me use Peter's circumstance to demonstrate this:

We can agree that Peter believed in Jesus, had a relationship with Jesus and he had faith. Being out in the raging sea Peter had no human resource to call upon to encourage him as the other disciples on the ship were equally scared.

Financial resources could not help him under those circumstances. His intellectual abilities could not help him. He could not come up with an idea to still the storm. Given Peter's circumstances he could only rely on his spiritual resources. Peter used his faith to walk on water and when he started sinking he prayed.

Prayer, exercise of his faith and the foreknowledge that Jesus never fails were all Peter had to use to his advantage. He did not attempt to swim which would have been one of his skills as a fisherman (he knew he would be courting death). I am sure all he thought about was that his survival was totally dependent on Jesus. Thank God for Peter and that raging storm. His experience serves to remind us that when we hit a state of hopelessness or cannot seem to identify any provision from

God that will help us to cope with our challenges, our faith in God is very profound in the midst of these circumstances. If you doubt the power of your faith read on:

So Jesus said to them, "Because of your unbelief; for assuredly, I say to you, if you have faith as a mustard seed, you will say to this mountain, 'Move from here to there,' and it will move; and nothing will be impossible for you."

~ Matthew 17:20

Read Matthew chapter 17 and you will understand the context in which Jesus made the statement. In your life, the mountain will be the challenges you face.

God is saying to us today, when our challenges appear insurmountable, exercise a tiny drop of faith (like a mustard seed) and there will be resolution. In other words challenges or problems will be solved.

I want you all to get into the habit when you face challenges to ask yourself the question:

What resources do I have available to cope with this challenge?

Let us do a quick review on the approach you should take to overcome your challenges.

The first thing to do is to list your resources: spiritual, financial, tangible (fixed assets), human (moral and spiritual support) and intellectual (ideas . . .). Having completed your list you need to ask yourself which one(s) will you need to use to help you?

Remember that you might not need to use all categories of resources. It will be dependent on the challenge you need to overcome.

OVERCOMING CHALLENGES

I will work through with you the use of your spiritual resource:

Spiritual resources are a prerequisite to problem solving so that resource should always be used in overcoming your challenges. Your next question should be which spiritual resource(s) do I need to use? Prayer is compulsory and God's Word reminds us:

> *Be anxious for nothing; but in everything by prayer and supplication with thanksgiving let your requests be made known to God.*
>
> *~ Philippians 4:6*

When you have made your request to God in prayer you have to show Him that you are serious about it. Some people ask God for His help but are not prepared to put out an effort to receive God's blessing. God expects us to persevere:

> *"So I say to you, ask, and it will be given to you; seek, and you will find; knock and it will be opened to you. For everyone who asks receives, and he who seeks finds, and to him who knocks it will be opened."*
>
> *~ St. Luke 11: 9–10*

You are the one facing your challenge so you need to determine what else, based on God's Word, you will need to do spiritually. Next, approach all the other resources in a similar manner, to the spiritual resources by identifying them and determining which one(s) is/are applicable. Using this approach, you are now ready to overcome any challenge that comes at you.

To reinforce the approach of resource reliance let us look at how the available resources were used to overcome challenges in the Old and New Testament.

THE WORD

The Old Testament tells us about a widow whose sons were about to be taken by the creditor as slaves in lieu of the debt she owed.

The first thing she did was to find the man of God, Elisha, and explain her dilemma to him:

> *A certain woman of the wives of the sons of the prophets cried out to Elisha, saying, "Your servant my husband is dead, and you know that your servant feared the Lord. And the creditor is coming to take my two sons to be his slaves."*
>
> *~2 Kings 4:1*

Remember in the Old Testament communication with God was done through His prophets or His angels.

You will agree that this widow, when faced with her challenge, applied her spiritual resource through Elisha the prophet. Interesting, but I won't comment yet. Let us read the next verse:

> *So Elisha said to her, "What shall I do for you? Tell me, what do you have in the house?" And she said, "Your maidservant has nothing in the house but a jar of oil."*
>
> *~2 Kings 4:2*

Now I will tell you what is interesting about this conversation between Elisha and the widow: Elisha asked her what he could do for her. He wanted to find out how he could help her with this outstanding debt. Follow me keenly. Elisha did not wait on her response as he quickly asked a second question in order to find out what resource she had available to help her.

Are you getting a clear picture of what was happening in that conversation? Let me explain, Elisha's first question encouraged the dependency syndrome, or the gift receiving mentality. This means that others solve your problem and you benefit from the solution. That is not what God expects from us as He wants us to use up the resources he has blessed us with and become active participants in the solution.

This is really getting more interesting. The widow's response gives me the impression that she really was expecting Elisha to solve her dilemma without making any contribution. Listen to her response again:

"Your maidservant has nothing in the house but a jar of oil."

Nothing, In other words this widow believed that this jar of oil was insignificant in helping her with her debt.

Have you ever regarded the resources that God has given to you as **nothing** when faced with what appears to be an insurmountable challenge? We are all guilty.

Elisha ignored her response; he never commented because her faith was about to be tested. Would she obey his instructions or would she ignore them based on her opinion of the resource that was available to her? Let us read on:

Then he said "Go, borrow vessels from everywhere, from all your neighbours – empty vessels; do not gather just a few. "And when you have come in you shall shut the door behind you and your sons; then pour it into all those vessels, and set aside the full ones." So she went from him and shut the door behind her and her sons, who brought the vessels to her and she poured it out.

~ 2 Kings 4: 3-5

Elisha was preparing her for a great miracle and so he told her to borrow empty vessels but he knew that she would have borrowed just a few vessels so he told her to borrow all the vessels she could get.

He also told her to shut the door behind her and her sons, pour the oil and set aside all the full vessels. The widow obeyed all the instructions given by Elisha and found that she had run out of vessels.

The widow was very obedient and went for further instruction from Elisha as so far, she had done all he had told her to do:

> *Then she came and told the man of God. And he said, "Go, sell the oil and pay your debt; and you and your sons live on the rest."*
>
> *~2 Kings 4:7*

Isn't it amazing how this widow thought that her jar of oil was nothing? This jar of oil through God's miraculous guidance paid her debt, took care of her future income and prevented her sons from becoming slaves.

Pause now and do your introspection . . . have you ever considered your God given resources as being inadequate to help you overcome challenges you face? Have you obeyed God in everything He has guided you to do?

Let us summarize the widow's approach in overcoming her challenges: she asked for spiritual help, identified her resource (jar of oil) had faith and was obedient in following the instructions given to her by Elisha.

When faced with challenges your tests become your testimony and your scars become your stars. Challenges are building blocks to a better relationship with God and opportunities for God's blessings, as reflected in the life of Job in the Old Testament.

OVERCOMING CHALLENGES

In examining the life of Job we read how Job lost all his material possessions, his health failed, but he held firmly to his faith despite these challenges. His wife on the other hand, lost her faith in God once the material possessions were taken away and her husband was no longer healthy. Job's wife did not even stop to assess her spiritual resource. Instead she told Job to curse God and die:

> *Then his wife said to him, "Do you still hold fast to your integrity? Curse God and die!"*
>
> *~Job 2: 9*

Are we like Job's wife when the challenges seem insurmountable? Cursing God is not the solution. As a matter of fact it intensifies your problem as you have stopped listening to God the problem solver and you would also have given up on your hope of eternal life.

Job, however, was aware that life would have challenges so things would not always be as he desired as indicated in his response to his wife:

> *But he said to her, "You speak as one of the foolish women speaks. Shall we indeed accept good from God, and shall we not accept adversity?' In all this Job did not sin with his lips."*
>
> *~Job 2:10*

I cannot recall seeing anything else mentioned in the Book of Job about his wife. Please examine your Bible with me to see if this is correct. Did she curse God and die? We will never know. What we do know, however, is that Job was more blessed after the challenges he faced than he was before:

THE WORD

Now the Lord blessed the latter days of Job more than his beginning; for he had fourteen thousand sheep, six thousand camels, one thousand yoke of oxen, and one thousand female donkeys. He also had seven sons and three daughters.

~ Job 42: 12-13

Let us now turn our attention to the New Testament and examine the first miracle that Jesus performed at the wedding in Cana of Galilee. Let me digress to make a quick reference to the earlier chapters on believing, relationship building and faith. To believe is a conscious decision taken by an individual. Relationship building and faith, on the other hand, are likely to take more time as persons learn and grow from each other and this happens too in our relationship with God.

Let us go back now to the wedding feast at Cana of Galilee. Remember this was Jesus' first miracle and no one had experienced His miracle working power before. This meant that believing would be a difficult task to achieve. There would be no one to confirm that Jesus had performed miracles prior to this. What was needed was someone who could attest in one way or another to the miracle working power of Jesus. The only person at the wedding feast who was qualified to do so would have been Jesus' mother. She knew her son and she knew that faith and obedience were key ingredients in receiving a miracle that would help to overcome the challenge faced at this wedding, the lack of wine. Jesus' mother did not give a one, two or three hour speech to convince those at the wedding of the need to be obedient to Jesus. Her approach was direct and her words concise:

His mother said to the servants, "Whatever he says to you, do it."

~ John 2:5

OVERCOMING CHALLENGES

Jesus and His disciples were invited guests to the wedding. I would imagine that the servants would know who Jesus was but not about his power to perform miracles. The servants, however, were obedient as they listened to what Jesus' mother had said:

> *Jesus said to them, "Fill the water pots with water," And they filled them up to the brim. And He said to them, "Draw some out now, and take it to the master of the feast." And they took it.*
>
> *~John 2: 7–8*

There was excitement at the wedding feast over the wine as it was the best. The disciples used this miracle to make a decision to believe in Jesus:

> *This beginning of signs Jesus did in Cana of Galilee, and manifested His glory, and His disciples believed in Him.*
>
> *~John 2: 11*

Thank God for Jesus' mother as there would have been no water turned into wine if she had not instructed the servants to be obedient. They believed her words and this was manifested in their actions.

Believing is a personal decision as previously mentioned. If you believe, you gain and if you doubt, you lose. The bride and groom would have lost out on having the best quality wine if their servants had not believed in the power of Jesus and filled up the water pots as He had instructed them to do. In addition, this couple would have had to live with the most embarrassing moment in their lives when their guests would have to be told:

"I know you are all having a good time and you are all awaiting the waiters to refill your glasses with wine but

THE WORD

mmmmmm . . . . Sorry!! We have no wine left . . . we did not know that all the persons we invited would have attended"

....
....
....

(This could have been a possible reason for the depletion of the wine. I leave you to state other reasons in the space provided).

I know at this point you all want to stop and think about how you dealt with previous challenges in your life. Before you do so let me go through another challenge experienced and overcame in the New Testament. A multitude had followed Jesus to a deserted place and He was moved with compassion and healed their sick. The disciples saw a challenge on their hands as it approached evening. These people were hungry in a deserted place and they did not want the responsibility of feeding them. How do I know?

> *When it was evening, his disciples came to Him, saying, "This is a deserted place, and the hour is already late. Send the multitude away, that they may go into the villages and buy themselves food."*
>
> *~ Matthew 14: 15*

These disciples were faced with stress and were distressed as they believed that it would be their responsibility to provide for these people. They thought that by being proactive they would escape this catering responsibility.

They, of all persons, should have known better than to be evasive with Jesus. There is always a lesson to be learnt. Let us find out more about this lesson:

OVERCOMING CHALLENGES

But Jesus said to them, "They do not need to go away. You give them something to eat."

~ Matthew 14: 16

Ha! The very thing that the disciples were afraid of happened – "You give them something to eat." How were the disciples going to handle this?

And they said to Him, "We have here only five loaves and two fish."

~ Matthew 14: 17

Note the choice of words, we have here only. In other words, the food available is inadequate and cannot feed a multitude. Are you getting the picture? Since the food was inadequate then the disciples hoped that Jesus would agree with their original plan to send the multitude away to buy themselves food. Did the disciples get their desired wish? Oh no! Instead Jesus asked for the food :

He said, "Bring them here to Me."

~ Matthew 14: 18

I can imagine how disappointed the disciples were to get that response. They, however, believed in the power of Jesus and had the faith to know that it was miracle time again so they obeyed Jesus. Let us look at how it all ended:

Then He commanded the multitudes to sit down on the grass. And He took the five loaves and the two fish, and looking up to heaven, he blessed and broke and gave the loaves to the disciples; and the disciples gave to the multitudes. So they all ate and were filled, and they took up twelve baskets full of the fragments that remained.

~ Matthew 14: 19-20

THE WORD

A multitude fed, and twelve baskets full of fragments remained. What a miracle! What were the resources that were used to perform this miracle? Five loaves, two fish and their faith in Jesus which translated into their obedience in doing what He requested of them. This action resulted in a miracle that fed over five thousand persons.

Jesus demonstrated a very vital act, that of thanksgiving. We should always remember to thank God for His provisions although these might appear inadequate to you based on your current needs. Jesus, in giving thanks to God for the five loaves and two fishes, demonstrated to us that our gratitude combined with God's miracle transforming power results in all our needs being taken care of.

The Old Testament and the New Testament have confirmed that challenges are a part of life and that there are resources provided by God that we can use to overcome them. Jesus offers some words of reassurance to us as we face our trials, a part of life's reality:

"These things I have spoken to you, that in Me you may have peace. In the world you will have tribulation; but be of good cheer, I have overcome the world."

John 16: 33

These words of comfort from Jesus are a reminder that life is not made up of a bed of rose petals only. There is also the stem of the rose which has a number of thorns which are painful when they pierce through the skin. The pain is a reminder that life has its fair share of challenges that hurt us, whether financially, emotionally or in some other way.

Jesus highlights the importance of peace and the absence of

turmoil which comes only through Him. As you face challenges and pause to assess the resources available to help you to overcome them, you need to be at peace. You will not be able to assess your resources if you are in turmoil, so focus on Jesus, The Prince of Peace, so that you will be able to assess your challenges calmly.

"Be of good cheer", hold on to God and ask for His guidance in helping you to identify the relevant resources to overcome your challenges. Your dark clouds will gradually fade to reveal your blue skies. Be patient and be peaceful as you use your God given resources. However, in order to overcome challenges I need to highlight that at times it might be necessary to accept a lowering of your 'status' as set by society's standard. Do not become overwhelmed by the thought of this, as when you fall, with God's help you will rise again. If you resist the need to make the necessary changes, you are likely to end up being worse off.

Here is an example:

You are the proud owner of a new car .... (name the vehicle of your choice in the space provided). You have received numerous compliments since you started driving this vehicle which translates into your being awarded a place by society's standard among the elite. You are 'riding high.'

The recession has reduced your income to such a level that it could result in foreclosure on your house, as your current income cannot accommodate both payments on the house and on the motor vehicle.

What would you do? Would you continue to struggle to meet the monthly payments on the car and the house until you lose both (the inevitable)? Or, would you recognize that you have to be prudent and lower your status by selling your vehicle and buying something cheaper or travel by bus or with friends for a while?

Some persons might want to pray for a miracle so that they can keep the car. I would like to remind you that God gives you wisdom and if you have to secure your house, then let go of the motor vehicle. This vehicle has become your idol and you need to remove it from your life before it destroys you. Put God first. I know, indeed, it is a humbling experience. Do not worry, as God will guide you so that in time you will be restored to your former status if it is His will. My point is, be practical. Reduce and eliminate whatever expenses you need to. Please do not worry about the opinion of others and allow this to prevent you from making adjustments to your status that are in your best interest:

> *Not that I speak in regard to need, for I have learned in whatever state I am, to be content: I know how to be abased, and I know how to abound. Everywhere and in all things I have learned both to be full and to be hungry, both to abound and to suffer need. I can do all things through Christ who strengthens me.*
>
> *~ Philippians 4: 11–13*

In relation to challenges that result in reducing our status, the real test is when we are able to use foresight to prepare for an inevitable fall (lowered status) and in like manner recognize when it is time to prepare to rise God's way (restored status).

When faced with challenges, always ask God to help you to use wisdom to determine if a changed status is required in your life. With patience, perseverance, your eyes focused on God and your ears attuned to His guidance, you will overcome. This might not necessarily happen in a short period of time as we usually expect but it will in God's perfect timing, so be patient.

In this period of recession we all face financial challenges of varying degrees but we also face other challenges such as relational with our partners, employers, co-workers..............
....
(include other challenges you face in the space provided).

An understanding of the importance of anger management and forgiveness dealt with in chapter 8 and 15 respectively will provide guidelines that will aid in overcoming relational challenges.

Please note, it is always important to start with your spiritual resource and ask God's guidance in selecting the other resources that will aid you in overcoming the challenge you face.

So, what is next? Get ready to be victorious when challenges arise.

– 7 –

Covetousness

Have you ever thought about how as human beings we always seem to desire some of the things that we see other persons with regardless of what we have?

All human beings have covetousness engrained in their DNA because of Adam's sin. Are you surprised? You know we are all descendants of Adam so perfection was replaced by the serpent's deception in Genesis chapter 3. I agree that the serpent beguiled Eve. Yes, he distorted the facts but Eve's desire to become like God enticed her to do exactly what the serpent suggested. Read on:

> *And the woman said to the serpent, "We may eat the fruit of the trees of the garden; but of the fruit of the tree which is in the midst of the garden, God has said 'You shall not eat it, nor shall you touch it, lest you die." Then the serpent said to the woman, "You will not surely die. For God knows that in the day you eat of it your eyes will be opened, and you will be like God, knowing good and evil."*
>
> *~ Genesis 3: 2–5*

The serpent knew that by eating the fruit Eve would become wise but this disobedience would mean a spiritual death, separation from God. The serpent did not explain clearly to Eve what the consequence would be of her action (the serpent lied).

Human beings by nature are not usually contented with what they have. Eve was no different and the serpent knew this:

> *So when the woman saw that the tree was good for food, that it was pleasant to the eyes, and a tree desirable to make one wise, she took of its fruit and ate. She also gave to her husband with her, and he ate.*
>
> *~ Genesis 3:6*

Covetousness is a sin. In order to avoid sinning, let us use Eve's experience with the serpent to look at some of the warning signals that can serve as reminders to us that we are approaching the 'danger line', covetousness.

Through Eve's experience we learnt that covetousness arises when we are desperate to have the things that someone else owns and we justify our actions by providing reasons that include:

- Satisfying a basic need (For Eve, it was food).
- Looks good (For Eve, the physical appearance of the fruit was appealing).
- Status (For Eve it was wisdom. In our time we would describe such an individual as an intellectual).

Let us now formalize the meaning of covetousness to see how it matches up with my assessment of Eve's action. According to *The Little Oxford Dictionary and Thesaurus*, to covet means to desire a thing belonging to another so we can agree that Eve was covetous.

THE WORD

When you are covetous your actions and desires (the sinful nature) are the driving force, and not obedience to God. Remember God knows our weaknesses and so He gives us His commandments to prevent us from sinning and ruining our relationship with Him and losing out on His ultimate gift to us of eternal life.

Read along with me:

"You shall not covet your neighbor's house; you shall not covet your neighbor's wife, nor his male servant, nor his female servant, nor his ox, nor his donkey, nor anything that is your neighbor's".

~ Exodus 20:17

God named specific things we should not covet. However, He knows that we are likely to covet other things and justify our actions by claiming that He had not made provisions for these. So there is the all inclusive provision, anything which means everything that belongs to your neighbour.

I am including one example in this category, your neighbour's husband. We have to be honest; females too are sometimes as guilty as the males in this respect.

The reasons highlighted for coveting your neighbour's husband are similar to the ones included in the example under your neighbour's wife.

Let me highlight at this point that when you are caught in the trap of covetousness, only God can free you when you make your confession to Him.

I will now examine each category in an effort to provide guidelines that will bring you into an awareness of some of the things that result in covetousness. You can make your personal list of other things you believe would lead to covetousness.

COVETOUSNESS

Before I begin let us do a quick review of the criteria for covetousness based on Eve's DNA:

- Satisfying a basic need
- Physically appealing
- Improved status

Your neighbour's house

A house is a basic need providing shelter. However, as human beings, we sometimes covet our neighbour's house because of the size of the house, architectural design and location.

You might have a beautiful apartment or townhouse but your neighbour might have a multi-storey house with a swimming pool, jacuzzi, tennis or badminton court with a private jogging trail overlooking the sea, or the lake.

Based on our analysis of Eve's covetousness your neighbours house satisfies the criteria for covetousness when:

- The house satisfies your need for shelter (that is the house you want to live in, not the one you currently occupy).
- The house would be appealing to the eyes because of its size, architectural design and other features.
- The status attached to your neighbour's house is shouting loud, 'Look at me I am affluent and I influence.' This house would be a status symbol. Your neighbour's house leaves you desperately desiring to possess it . . . now!

Be contented with your house and give thanks to God for your blessings as well as your neighbour's.

Your neighbour's wife

Oh, how you wish you could boast about her and have her as your own:

- She would satisfy your need for companionship.
- She is appealing to the eyes, she's beautiful. She has the most perfect shape you have ever seen so close up (of course you see the shapely ones on the movie screen daily).
- Status? Yes, of course, she is dynamic and educated. The perfect wife, representing your success and family stability.

Please be faithful to your partner and appreciate God's gift to you. Thank God for your wife and join your neighbour in giving thanks for his wife without being covetous.

Your neighbour's male servant

Why would you envy your neighbour's male servant?

- The male servant/employee would satisfy your need for help to perform tasks in your business or home.
- He could be appealing to the eye, in that based on his physique he would be strong enough to help with these tasks. On the other hand, his recommendation could be impressive based on his experience. You are the one who determines the factors for appealing based on your criteria.
- Regarding status, your success to some degree would be dependent on a reliable male servant/employee who would therefore be an asset to you resulting in the growth of your business. Instead of coveting your neighbour for his male servant ask God to help you to find the right person that will compliment your business or household.

COVETOUSNESS

Your neighbour's female servant

- Your female helper would satisfy your need for assistance in the day to day running of the home. In these days a good servant or helper aids the family in so many ways. This person ensures that meals are prepared for the family, the laundry and shopping are done. Most importantly where there are children in the family, the helper takes care of them.

- She may be appealing to the eyes depending on what you are looking for. A family with young children might want a young person that the children can play with. On the other hand, another family might want an older person to assume the role of grandmother to the children.

- Status is maintained as you are able to work since there is a reliable helper to take care of your family. Where status entails entertaining on a large scale a good helper is vital along with your caterers and event planners in maintaining your image as a host/hostess.

In these times when a good female helper is difficult to find the temptation is to covet but remember God's Word, it is wrong. What you need to do is to persist in your efforts to find a helper and ask God to help you to choose the right person.

Your neighbour's Ox

From a Biblical perspective, the ox would be the animal used for work, which was primarily farming in those days. In our context today, in addition to farming, work would include manufacturing and service industries. Include the nature of your work in the space provided ....

In today's world, the ox then would be equivalent to vehicles or machines used for work purposes. Include the type of vehicle/machine you need for your work............................

Do not covet your neighbour's vehicle/machinery based on the nature of your work. There are reasons, however, that you believe justify your desire for your neighbours's vehicle/machinery:

- It satisfies your need at this point as it is new and you can operate efficiently without worrying about maintenance costs. Include other ways in which this vehicle/machinery satisfies your need. ....

- The vehicle/machinery is appealing to your eyes its metallic colors and additional features. Include other ways in which the vehicle/ machinery would be appealing to you Status? ....

- Yes! That vehicle/ machinery in your business is definitely a status symbol. Not many persons would be able to afford it ....

(Include other reasons in the space provided that would justify this vehicle/machinery being regarded as a status symbol).

Admire but do not covet your neighbour's vehicle/machinery. Work hard, give thanks to God and wait on His guidance and blessings.

Your neighbour's donkey

From a biblical perspective the donkey would be like the family vehicle. In today's world, we would use .... (Please include your personal taste in the space provided). Let us look at some of the reasons that could lead to covetousness:

- It satisfies your need for an expensive vehicle or ....
(Include other reasons in the space provided).
- This vehicle is appealing to the eyes with all the additional features it has or ....
(Include other reasons in the space provided).
- Status? Definitely! Not many persons can afford this vehicle and so it would serve to identify you with the elite..
(Include other reasons in the space provided).

Anything that is you neighbour's

I have repeated the reasons for covetousness which are similar to the ones included under Your neighbour's wife.

Your neighbour's husband. Oh, how you wish you could boast about him and have him as your own:

- He would satisfy your need for companionship.
- He looks good, he is appealing to the eyes, he is handsome. He is muscular . . . just look at his biceps and triceps . . . He has the most perfect body you have ever seen so close up (of course, you see the muscular males on the movie screen).
- Status? Yes, of course, his leadership style is unique and he excels on the job. He is the perfect husband, representing your success and family stability.

Please be faithful to your partner and appreciate God's gift to you. Thank God for your husband and join your neighbour in giving thanks for hers without being covetous. The mere fact that God warns us not to be covetous is an indication that it will cause harm in our human interpersonal relationships which could include death. Let us now examine the impact of covetousness in three instances in the Bible.

David and Bathsheba

David, the king of Judah, was looking through his window one day and he saw Bathsheba, this beautiful lady the wife of Uriah, having her bath:

> *Then it happened one evening that David arose from his bed and walked on the roof of the king's house. And from the roof he saw a woman bathing, and the woman was very beautiful to behold.*
>
> *~2 Samuel 11:2*

David immediately sent for Bathsheba to satisfy his sexual desires and then he sent her back to her matrimonial home. Unfortunately, what he was not bargaining for happened, as she sent a message to let him know she was pregnant! He coveted his neighbor's wife and now it has really gotten complex. So what did he do? He tried to persuade Uriah, to go home and sleep with his wife so that the pregnancy could appear to have been caused by him. That did not work as Uriah was a faithful soldier and thought it would be unfair for him to go home and cuddle up with his wife while his co-workers were on the battle field.

When king David saw that his plan did not work, he arranged for Uriah to be placed at the head of the battle so that he would be killed (2 Samuel 11: 14-15).

Covetousness resulted in the death of Uriah the Hittite husband.

COVETOUSNESS

David then married Bathsheba but God was not pleased and so God killed the baby that was born from their 'covetous marital' relationship. God was merciful, however, as he forgave David and blessed their second child, Solomon, who became the richest and wisest man in the world.

Ahab and Naboth's vineyard

Ahab, king of Samaria, wanted a vineyard that was near to his palace in Jezreel. He approached the owner Naboth, who refused to sell it as it was an inheritance from his family. So, Ahab coveted Naboth's vineyard.

I reminded you previously that disobedience to God by being covetous can be fatal. In an effort to get this vineyard, Jezebel, Ahab's wife arranged to kill Naboth. How did this end? God was displeased, and so Ahab and Jezebel died under circumstances not befitting a king or his queen (1 Kings 21: 17–20).

Covetousness resulted in not only the death of Naboth but also Ahab and Jezebel.

The Parable of the Talents

You might not have interpreted the behaviour of the servant who was given one talent as being covetous, but let us examine the story together to find out what really happened:

A man travelling to a far country gave three of his servants some talents to invest until he returned. One of the servant got five, another two and the third, one. The third servant, with the one talent, coveted the talents of the other two servants. In addition, it appeared as if that servant also coveted his boss resources based on some of the things he said:

THE WORD

Then he who had received the one talent came and said, 'Lord, I knew you to be a hard man, reaping where you have not sown, and gathering where you have not scattered seed. 'And I was afraid, and went and hid your talent in the ground. Look, there you have what is yours.

~ Matthew 25: 24–25

Covetousness drove this servant to inactivity. He could have put the money on deposit and earned some interest as the master had suggested:

So you ought to have deposited my money with the bankers and at my coming I would have received back my own with interest.

~ Matthew 25: 27

Imagine, if the servant had deposited the money in the bank, his master would have entrusted him with more assets as he did with the other servants:

For to everyone who has, more will be given, and he will have abundance; but from him who does not have, even what he has will be taken away.

~ Matthew 25: 29

Unfortunately, the servant settled for covetousness and lost everything:

Therefore take the talent from him, and give it to him who has ten talents.

~ Matthew 25:28

If you have been covetous or know someone who has been. Did you or that person experience some personal loss through that selfish desire to want what another person has?

We now understand clearly that covetousness can lead to the demise of others and to inactivity in our lives. Look back at the examples of king David and Bathsheba, king Ahab, Jezebel and Naboth and the parable of the talents. Murder was the end result in the first two instances, and inactivity and a waste of human talent was the end result in the third. God wants us to avoid these things and so he commands us not to be covetous.

I want you to be clear on the meaning of covetousness. God wants us to strive for things honestly and without guile, so that he gets the glory. Remember, it is okay to strive for things that are similar to your neighbour's. On the other hand, you are covetous when you desire the things that already belong to your neighbour. An example will reinforce the point:

If you look at your neighbour's car and decide that it is worth having one like it, for genuine reasons such as fuel efficiency, resale value...

....

(include other reasons in the space provided) that is acceptable. However, If you want your neighbour's car then you are being covetous.

God wants us to love one another, be happy for the success of others and enjoy our blessings. Be contented with what you have and who you are. Acceptance of self helps you to avoid covetousness.

He also wants us to understand that in order to avoid covetousness, the quality of our lives should not be dependent on material acquisitions:

And He said to them, "Take heed and beware of covetousness, for one's life does not consist in the abundance of the things he possesses."

~ Luke 12:15

– 8 –

Anger

As human beings from time to time we express our feelings of anger verbally or with our facial expression and body language. So, what is anger? Anger is an emotion, it is a warning signal that you have been hurt. Anger is usually expressed by degrees, moving from being slightly annoyed and progressing to a fit of rage. At that stage, an individual may be described as irrational because of the things said or done.

The stages in anger are best described by comparing it to an electric kettle. In preparation for boiling, water is poured into the electric kettle at room temperature. The water heats gradually until it reaches boiling point. The electric kettle has a built in control, so that once the water reaches boiling point the kettle automatically turns off. We too have a built in control that triggers warning signals and alerts us when we are getting angry. Our warning signals include sweaty palms, headaches, a desire to punch or kick, swearing or a desire to swear. Include your warning signals in the space provided.............
.........................Once we are alerted by our warning signals, we know we are getting angry. We then should consciously make an effort to control our anger.

ANGER

On the other hand, there is the other kettle that we use on the stove which does not have a built in control to automatically turn it off when it reaches boiling point.

This kettle whistles to alert us that the water has reached boiling point. However, if the kettle is not removed from the source of heating then the water will continue to boil and then spew uncontrollably from its spout.

Similarly, most of us tend to behave like the whistling kettle without the built in control when it reaches boiling point so that we spew our anger uncontrollably at others and consequently destroy our relationship with them.

We know that anger is an emotion. The question is, how did we get this emotion that can be so destructive when uncontrolled? Your respone..
....

It is a part of our emotional makeup, given to us by God in whose image we have all been made. God, our heavenly Father, gets angry, but He controls it:

The Lord is merciful and gracious, slow to anger and abounding in mercy.

~ Psalms 103:8

Please note, God is slow to anger.
When does God get angry with us? Your response..............
....

God gets angry with us when we are disobedient and do things that are evil in His sight:

God is a just judge, and God is angry with the wicked every day.

~ Psalm 7:11

THE WORD

So far we should all agree that the problem is not in getting angry, but allowing our anger to be destructive and hurt others physically, emotionally, verbally and................................... (list other ways you have hurt others in the space provided).

The Bible attests to the fact that anger is a natural emotion:

Be angry, and do not sin: do not let the sun go down on your wrath.

~ Ephesians 4:26

The aforementioned verse is helping us to understand that it is okay to express anger, but the extent to which we do so will determine whether we have sinned by our actions towards our fellow human beings.

Why do we react so badly when we are angry? Your response
....

We take everything personally, meaning that our primary focus is on ourselves. We believe that every word and action is said or done to belittle, criticize or offend us. We are unable to even accept that we need to understand the context as well as the perspective from which the other person's statements or comments have been made. In other words, we tend to be subjective instead of being objective in our assessment of our conflicts.

This is natural, as human beings tend to be self-centred and not God-centred.

What is the difference? Your response...............................

Self-centered persons see only the hurt or wrong that has been done to them and are not concerned about the things that could have impacted the other persons' lives resulting in their current behaviour.

God centered persons, however, see those who have hurt

ANGER

them as needing help and so are more concerned about the needs of others than themselves. Such persons allow themselves to be receptive to God's guidance in order to help others:

Bless those who persecute you; bless and do not curse.

~ Romans 12:14

The example below will illustrate the difference between a self-centred and a God-centred person:

- Your child was rude to you in the presence of your employees and you were embarrassed.

- When you got home you physically or verbally abused your child. This happened because you were self-centered, you were more focused on your feelings of embarrassment than on helping your child to learn and grow from the experience.

How could you have dealt with the matter using a God-centred approach?

Your response..
....

You would have asked yourself, 'What has led my child to behave this way in public?' In providing answers to this question you would:

- Explore with your child how he or she was feeling at the time of the incident. Find out from your child if something happened before the incident that might have triggered that behaviour. Ask the Holy Spirit to help you to be compassionate as you guide your child in understanding his or her behaviour that demonstrated disrespect towards you. If this incident is not the first time your child has behaved this way in public, you need to remind your child of his or her conduct in the past. Help your child to understand that an apology is needed and that you will remove some privilege temporarily that the child enjoys to demonstrate that the behaviour was unacceptable and should not be repeated.

Please do not scream and shout at the child as 'scare tactics' will not teach the child the valuable lesson of respect and obedience. Your action will only instill fear. Yes, the child's behaviour may improve because of fear but not from a positive value learnt from you. Hence the inappropriate behaviour is likely to continue with others.

Would you have dealt with the scenario in the manner I suggested? You may not be at that place, as yet. However, you have an opportunity to strive to get there with God's help. The emphasis is on striving; it is hard work to make changes in our lives. When you pray, ask God to help you to be God-centred.

Now that we have examined the God and self-centred approaches, I have one question for you:

Are you willing to accept that we should think of others and not take everything personally? Remember we are expected to please God:

> *Be kindly affectionate to one another with brotherly love, in honor giving preference to one another.*
>
> **Romans 12:10**

From now on I hope you will accept that at least some of the hurt you experience because of some persons means that something in their past or current life, which you do not know anything about, could have accounted for their angry outbursts/reaction. Let us always remember the commandment of Jesus to love one another:

ANGER

This is My commandment, that you love one another as I have loved you.

~ John 15:12

Love means giving rather than receiving:

For God so loved the world that He gave His only begotten Son, that whoever believes in Him should not perish but have everlasting life.

~ John 3:16

When situations cause us to be angry, this means our giving should entail: empathy, compassion, and kindness in both words and deeds.

Include your comments in the space provided......................

....

....

Have you written your comments?

I am sure you will agree with me that your life is to be used for the glory of God and so you must aim to live by God's standard.

The hurt feelings you experienced because of your anger provides an opportunity for you to learn, as you use these experiences to glorify God by your actions towards others.

If the God-centered approach to anger is practised, I am sure there would be less murder and domestic violence in our world.

Once we realize the importance of obedience to God, we will be more willing to forgive others who have caused us to be angry in the past, and be even willing to reconcile with them.

To support this point let us look at what Jesus had to say on reconciliation:

THE WORD

Therefore if you bring your gift to the altar, and there remember that your brother has something against you, leave your gift there before the altar, and go your way. First be reconciled to your brother, and then come and offer your gift.

~ Matthew 5:23-24

Finding out from an individual how you have offended him or her is a very humiliating experience. If you are self-centred, your pride will prevent you from doing so. It is only the God-centred approach that will help us to act humbly, enabling us to consult with others in an effort to resolve our conflicts. We have been informed that visualization techniques (imagining calming scenarios like the beach, listening to one's favorite music) and exercise (yoga, aerobics, punching bags) will help us to manage our anger. However, God has guided us in His Word as to how we can reduce or even avoid anger in our relationships with others. Remember in many instances harsh words are triggered in anger and God who knows us best cautions us against this:

A soft answer turns away wrath, But a harsh word stirs up anger.

~ Proverbs 15:1

I beseech you to start, initially, with one day (twenty-four hours) and practise the approach of Jesus by using 'gentle words', and think about the needs of others as you face situations that are likely to cause anger.

Once you apply this method, you will see that when you are hurt by others you will be able to look to Jesus, The Prince of Peace, for guidance in doing what is right. It is also important for you to acknowledge that change takes time so do not get frustrated and cease your efforts in managing your anger.

However, if you find yourself regressing at times to your old behaviour, do not hesitate to ask Jesus, our Prince of Peace, to guide you to do what is pleasing in His sight.

Always bear in mind that your life on earth is preparing you for eternity and anger and strife are deterrent to a life with Jesus. It is therefore important to apply the guideline provided in the Word of God:

Be angry and do not sin: do not let the sun go down on your wrath.

~ Ephesians 4:26

– 9 –

Pride

When someone describes another person as proud, is that necessarily a bad thing?

Include your opinion in the space provided..........................

In my opinion, it is good when persons are pleased with their achievements in a 'healthy way'. This means that they are satisfied with the results derived from their efforts.

God wants us to display a 'healthy' pride in our lives and demonstrates this in His response to the things He created:

> *Then God saw everything that He made, and indeed it was very good. So the evening and the morning were the sixth day.*
>
> *~ **Genesis 1:31***

However, God is displeased when we display pride in 'unhealthy ways' to each other. How do we display unhealthy pride? The remainder of this chapter will focus on this. People sometimes find themselves surrounded by persons who treat them as if they are beneath their dignity or act in a condescending manner towards them (as superior relating to inferior). Pride then is when persons demonstrate by their actions that they consider themselves to be better than others.

The 'P' in pride denotes power as these persons believe they have authority or control over others.

The Word of God confirms that persons do display power when they are proud:

> *I will break the pride of your power; I will make your heavens like iron and your earth like bronze.*
>
> ~ *Leviticus 26:19*

This passage serves as a reminder that God is not pleased with us when we are proud. His displeasure with us results in consequences as God explained to the children of Israel:

> *And your strength shall be spent in vain; for your land shall not yield its produce, nor shall the trees of the land yield their fruit.*
>
> ~ *Leviticus 26:20*

How do we see pride demonstrated in our society today?

Persons who exhibit pride demonstrate control over those they aim to convince of their superior position. However, Jesus warns us of the dangers of being proud:

> *Pride goes before destruction, and a haughty spirit before a fall.*
>
> ~ *Proverbs 16:18*

Pride is indeed destructive in that it affects our relationship with God and our interpersonal relationships with each other. Ultimately, we suffer (destruction) as reminded in God's Word.

It is evident that God is not pleased with persons who are proud. Nebuchadnezzar, the king of Babylon was humbled by God for his pride and attested to the need for us as human beings to acknowledge God as our Creator and avoid pride:

THE WORD

Now I, Nebuchadnezzar, praise and extol and honor the King of heaven, all of whose works are truth, and His ways justice. And those who walk in pride He is able to put down.

~ Daniel 4:37

Take some time to read Daniel chapter 4 to learn more about the consequences of Nebuchadnezzar's pride. When we are blessed by God we should not be proud as our blessings are not given to elevate us above others. Instead, we are expected to share our talents, abilities and financial resources in whatever ways we can with others without being proud.

The stereotyping in our society sometimes results in some persons demonstrating a sense of pride in their career over others who are not as recognized. Some of the persons that our society recognizes as important include doctors, lawyers and nurses as these persons are looked upon as playing an important role. Others however, disregard the garbage collectors, household helpers and other persons who are deemed to be less important by the standard of our society. Have you ever stopped to think what our world would be like without these persons in the category of the 'disregarded'?

Can you imagine a few weeks without garbage collectors? Garbage would remain uncollected. Can you imagine the stench (ugh! ugh!) And the likelihood of diseases.

What about life without the household helpers? (As the name suggests these persons are there to help us and not to do everything for us). Without helpers it would be more difficult for parents who work to ensure that their children are taken care of. Getting home in the evenings after work could mean not having a home cooked meal awaiting you as well as an immaculate house.

I hope these examples serve to demonstrate that our roles might be different but they are all important in enabling us to live together on planet earth.

If we have been guilty by thinking of ourselves as better than others because of our achievements, let us now stop and ask God to help us to understand and appreciate that we have different roles in life.

We should never forget that in one way or another we all need each other (if you have not yet discovered this, you might be surprised soon).

Please stop and do your introspection on pride by providing responses to the questions below:

- If life is no longer kind to you and you find yourself in a position less than you are accustomed to, would you be happy if, in your changed status, someone behaves proudly and leaves you feeling belittled?

- Do the proud breathe a special air or is it the same air that God has provided for all of us to breathe?

- Do the proud have a special blood that runs through their veins or is the composition of the blood similar for all of us?

- Will the proud die like all of us or are they the exception?

- Is there a guarantee in life that you will always have or be able to use the things that cause you to be proud?

- Did Jesus exclude the proud from His commandment to love one another?

As you ponder on pride and its damaging effect in your lives, your interpersonal and spiritual relationships; I have provided an acronym to highlight common areas where pride is exhibited in our lives:

Physical Appearance – Includes hair type, skin colour. Many persons see these differences as reasons to see themselves as being better than others.

Riches – Some wealthy persons believe that being affluent gives them the right to disregard those who cannot live in elaborate homes or drive expensive cars.

Intellect – There are persons who regard others as unintelligent and become impatient in their presence when these persons are unable to relate at their level.

Dressing – Some persons can afford to dress well and sometimes see others as inferior to them as their financial resource is a limiting factor that prevents them from adhering to an acceptable dress code.

Earned Status – There are persons from affluent family heritage who believe that this gives them the right to act in a superior manner to others who have no such association.

Whatever we are born with or achieve in life are all gifts from God to be used to His glory and we are all equal in his sight despite our differences in race, social or economic status.

When we exhibit pride in the areas highlighted above or in other areas this leads to destructive behaviour. This can be expressed using an acronym as:

POWER

RIDE

INTENT ON

DESTROYING YOUR

ETERNAL LIFE WITH GOD

When you are tempted to be proud think on these things which in many instances results in the humiliation of others. Instead of displaying pride, recognize that you are privileged to be alive. With our gratitude to God for life, let us joyfully and respectfully love and serve our fellow human beings:

For you brethren, have been called to liberty; only do not use liberty as an opportunity for the flesh, but through love serve one another.

~ Galatians 5:13

Jesus could justifiably have been proud as the Son of God. Instead, He came here on earth and allowed us to crucify Him in a humiliating manner in order to pay the price for our sins so that ultimately we would be able to enjoy eternal life. So let us treat others with respect and use our blessings to the glory of God:

Therefore whatever you want men to do to you, do also to them, for this is the Law and the Prophets.

~ Matthew 7:12

Are you ready to make the changes in your life now?

−10−

Humility

Humility reflects one's modest behavior or response in a given situation, determined by that individual's perspective on life.

Do you agree? If you do not, include your opinion in the space provided ....

A humble person, then, is one who is not proud because of academic, material or birth status (member of family dynasty) and .... (include your suggestions in the space provided).

Let us now look at some of the ways humble persons treat others in their interaction with them:

Accept others are as they are (rich, poor, ... (include other ways in the space provided).

Do not attempt to impress others in order to be recognized.

Treat others with respect and do not belittle or ostracize anyone.

Humble persons through their interaction with others demonstrate the way God wants us to relate to each other.

Never forget that God does not want us to be attention seekers based on our clothes, academic qualifications or other things ....(include the list of things in the space provided that prevents you or others from being humble).

God loves to see His children humble, as His Word declares:

> *But He gives more grace. Therefore He says: "God resists the proud, but gives grace to the humble."*
>
> *~James 4:6*

To understand what genuine humility is, let us now look at Jesus and the circumstances He faced and how He dealt with them.

Status by Birth

Jesus is the Son of God, which means all that God, His Father, has belongs to Him. He did not have to come here and have His birth place in a manger amongst the animals. God could have provided a palace for the birth of His only Son.

Jesus did not see our human condition as being beneath His dignity. He accepted it in order to identify with us, as He loves us.

There is nowhere in the Bible that Jesus expresses regret at coming to earth to live under our conditions.

Relating to Sinners

Jesus related to all sinners including tax collectors, the poor and needy. He ate and drank with them, not deeming himself better than them. Jesus was not applauded for His actions; instead He was criticized. Read what Jesus had to say:

> *The Son of Man came eating and drinking, and they say, 'Look, a glutton and a winebibber, a friend of tax collectors and sinners!' But wisdom is justified by her children.*
>
> *~Matthew 11:19*

Physical contact with a sinner

Would you have a sinner wash your feet with her tears and have that stigma attached to your name?

> *And behold, a woman in the city who was a sinner, when she knew that Jesus sat at the table in the Pharisee's house, brought an alabaster flask of fragrant oil, and stood at His feet behind Him weeping; and she began to wash His feet with her tears and wiped them with the hair of her head; and she kissed His feet and anointed them with the fragrant oil.*
>
> ~ Luke 7:37–38

Read the comments made by the Pharisee who had invited Jesus to dine when He allowed this woman to wash his feet:

> *Now when the Pharisee who had invited Him saw this, he spoke to himself saying, "This Man, if He were a prophet, would know who and what manner of woman this who is touching Him, for she is a sinner."*
>
> ~ Luke 7:39

Residence

Jesus had no residence that was in keeping with His status as the Son of God. In fact, He did not even own a house:

> *Now it happened as they journeyed on the road, that someone said to Him, "Lord, I will follow You wherever You go." And Jesus said to him, "Foxes have holes and birds of the air have nests, but the Son of Man has nowhere to lay His head."*
>
> ~ Luke 9: 57–58

Respect

Jesus faced insults and rejection, yet He remained respectful and never retaliated or flaunted His Divine power.

HUMILITY

We should all strive to model in our daily living the humility that Jesus demonstrated in relating to others. Many times, however, when persons are humble, their actions are mistaken for weakness.

What do I mean by this? Let me demonstrate this with a scenario:

A lawyer has been verbally abused by the cashier in a supermarket. The lawyer resolved the conflict in a respectful manner with the cashier without disclosing his identity. Include your comment on the lawyer's action in the space provided..

....

Some persons would have expected the lawyer to flaunt his status and threaten to take legal action.

The fact that the lawyer resolved the conflict amicably without self disclosure would be deemed by some persons as a sign of weakness.

Include situations where you have experienced or observed humility being mistaken for weakness in the space provided.

....

....

This example with the lawyer serves to remind us that we should always bear in mind that our actions should not be based on the crowd's response or expectations, but on a deeper knowledge of what God wants us to do.

Okay, here are some questions for you. In the blank spaces, please provide responses with explanations where necessary that will indicate your level of humility:

THE WORD

- How easy is it for you to say, 'I am sorry'?
  ....
  ....

- How would you respond if a co-worker highlights your mistakes and guides you in correcting these?
  ....
  ....

- Would you find it easy to commend a co-worker whose brilliant idea has been implemented by the organization?
  ....
  ....

- How would you respond if your child highlights the negative impact of your conduct and corrects you?
  ....
  ....

- If you were ignored in a situation where you should have received recognition for your status would you irately or humbly inform the offending party of the oversight?
  ....
  ....

Having examined the life of Jesus as our model of humility, why is it so difficult for us as human beings to be humble?
Let's explore some reasons together:

- As human beings, we generally feel that there is a need to be recognized as persons of worth by others.

- We use the society's criteria to determine what or who is accepted and use this to guide us in seeking validation.

HUMILITY

- We sometimes become so desperate in our need for acceptance that we believe if we do not draw the world's attention to us, we will go into oblivion (no one will remember we exist unless we tell them we still do).

As a result, our actions demonstrate our belief that everyone is acknowledging others, but not us, and we too need to be seen and recognized.

However, humility comes unannounced with a calmness that does not beg for the world's attention.

If we come to that place where we know who we are in Christ, we will recognize that we are all made in the image of God. We will also learn to appreciate our diversity as we are from different races and cultures with physical features uniquely made by God.

In addition, our individual talents and abilities should not be viewed as greater than or less than those of other persons. Instead, our talents and abilities are all needed to make this world a better place.

If we believe God's Word and live accordingly, there is no doubt that we will all remain humble.

I implore you all to look at your lives and to see if any achievements or physical attributes have made you think of yourself as better than others. If so, let us all strive to be humble.

Below I have provided you with the acronym HUMBLE which will give you examples of characteristics that a humble person should display. As you read, assess your own life and share the acronym with others:

THE WORD

Humane – Recognizing that we are all God's children and we need to care for one another. We need to respect each other regardless of class, race and economic status. God also commands us to be kind to one another:

> And be kind to one another, tenderhearted, forgiving one another, even as God in Christ forgave you.
>
> *~ Ephesians 4:32*

Understanding – Be willing to empathize with the needs, pains and sorrows of others. We should also be willing to rejoice with those who are happy, strive to understand and help persons with low self esteem and those who are insecure with their social interactions with others.

Modest – Not allowing academic or other achievements, physical beauty or material acquisitions to precede you by drawing attention to these things through your behaviour or mannerisms. In other words, do not be ostentatious (Do not show off!).

Barrier Remover – A change agent who demonstrates and encourages others not to discriminate regardless of class, race or economic status. We should encourage persons not to patronize or treat others as inferiors but instead be respectful to everyone.

Loving – A genuine concern for the well being of others. A willingness to be unselfish achieved by helping others. Whatever is done to help others should not be done solely for public applause or recognition but should be done genuinely in the interest of those who need our help.

Let me repeat, the humble person does not boast about the ways they have assisted others so that their good deeds become public knowledge to gain accolades. Instead, when these persons speak they do so in a manner that encourages others to give.

Jesus discourages giving solely for public recognition:

Therefore when you do a charitable deed, do not sound a trumpet before you as the hypocrites do in the synagogues and in the streets, that they may have glory from men. Assuredly, I say to you, they have their reward.

~ Matthew 6:2–4

Enduring – Or being patient, is one of the hallmarks of the humble person. These persons recognize that changes and growth take time and so they understand the virtue of patience in their lives as well as in their relationship with others.

Jesus as our role model of humility demonstrated love in everything He did. In obedience to God, let us follow the example of Jesus.

- It is time for self-examination . . .
- Are you loving and lovable?
- Are you humble?

Please read this chapter again and where possible make the changes in your life that God expects of you:

Therefore humble yourselves under the mighty hand of God, that He may exalt you in due time.

~ 1 Peter 5:6

– 11 –

Patience

Waiting is not the easiest thing, yet our failure to do so has an adverse impact on our lives.

So then, what are some of the things that cause us to become impatient? Let us work these through together:

- Making decisions by weighing the pros and cons, that is, the advantages and disadvantages that are likely based on the action taken.
- The desire to achieve long-term goals in the short-term.
- The uncertainty about the outcome of decisions to be made in the future.
- Fear of repetition of the results relating to past experiences on current decisions.

Your personal reasons for not being patient.

....
....
....

Whatever the reasons are, I am sure you will agree that your actions are guided by your impulses ('I need to act now!'). As human beings, our impulsive actions are usually based on our desires that are driven without reasoning.

What we all need to do before we act impulsively is to apply reasoning to the circumstance we face and make our decisions accordingly.

Let me share with you some steps you can follow when you are feeling impatient and you believe a decision needs to be made urgently.

Ask yourself:

- Why am I feeling impatient?

State your reasons

....
....

These reasons could include past experiences and uncertainty about the future. There are times too when persons are in denial because of incidents that have caused them to be impatient and find it difficult to accept the reality of the impact on their lives. In addition, some persons repress their experiences and find it difficult to recall these incidents. Exercising patience is important in recalling incidents that have occurred in the past. If you patiently reflect I am confident that you will recall.

Based on your response to the question above you need to do an honest assessment:

Are these reasons justified? For example, should I really be impatient because of what happened to me in the past? (Using the assumption that your reason above is based on past experience). Include your assessment for your impatience in the space provided: ....
....

THE WORD

Be careful how you allow your past experience to prevent you from exercising patience in the future.

Past experiences do not necessarily have to repeat themselves. If you are getting impatient because of a past experience, analyse carefully what had happened and learn from it. Let me use an example with suggested responses to demonstrate this:

Your boss encouraged you to apply for a job in the organization which would be a promotion for you. He convinced you that you would get the job but unfortunately you did not. A year later, there has been another job offer and you apply on your own initiative. A week later, you realize that another employee in your department has applied. You fear rejection again based on the fact that you did not get the job previously. You decide to send in your resignation because you believe that other person in your department will get the job. Stop! Reason this through:

Step 1

Ask yourself the question:
- Why did the other person get the first job your boss referred you to and not you?

Perhaps the person was more qualified or had more experience.

Step 2

Ask yourself the question:
- What do you need to do?

You could go back to school to upgrade your qualification or get more on-the-job training.

At this stage do not think of walking away from your job, as you would be giving up years of service in a stable work environment. In light of the current recession you might not have the stability in a new job.

Step 3

Ask yourself the question:

- Is there a lesson that God wants me to learn through this experience?

If yes, it could be a lesson to build my character which will provide a testimony for others If no, what should I do?

Answers to your 'no' response above could be provided through prayer and reading your Bible.

Look at the experience of some of the Bible characters, and note what they learnt through these tests of patience. In addition, you could seek advice from someone trustworthy who you know has experienced several tests in patience. Sometimes God uses our fellow human beings to help us:

Bear one another's burdens, and so fulfill the law of Christ.

~ Galatians 6:2

Step 4

Ask yourself the question:

- Will this experience provide the foundation for other challenges I will face?

This could be a wake-up call to the reality of the inevitable, life's tests or challenges, as Jesus said:

"In the world you shall have tribulation be of good cheer I have overcome the world."

~ John 16:33

Now that you have practised the steps in dealing with how to cope with the impact of a past experience, let us now look at the approach you can take when faced with experiences that test your patience repeatedly.

Tests on patience will always be a part of life's experience. The ability to cope will depend on how you handle being tested repeatedly. If you learn from subsequent experiences, when challenged you will not be impulsive but will learn instead to wait on God. Let us now examine the steps you should take when tested repeatedly:

Step A

Ask yourself the question:

- Have I learnt anything new from being repeatedly tested?

If the answer is 'yes', then there is the likelihood that there are further lessons to be learnt when faced with challenges that require patience as part of the solution. In other words, if you had mastered all possible lessons in patience there would be nothing new to learn from this experience.

If the answer is 'no', then, reassess the experience to see if you have overlooked any new lesson.

If after you have done so, you still have not learnt anything new, then move on to Step B.

Step B

Ask yourself the question:

- What do I need to do now?

Prove that you can handle current challenges that are testing your patience, by dealing with them appropriately as they arise.

If you are unable to deal with your challenges patiently then

PATIENCE

you need to review all the steps (1-4) highlighted above to determine what you did not master.

I hope the aforementioned suggestions will help you to be more patient in the future.

Let us test what you have learnt about patience by examining the scenario below:

- You have a boss that is abusive, and because you have been patient in dealing with his conduct by responding politely you have learnt restraint:

A soft answer turns away wrath, but a harsh word stirs up anger.

~ Proverbs 15:1

- You have experienced years of abuse from your boss. You believe you are not learning anything new from these repeated abuses. You cannot reason with your boss. He is adamant and arrogant. You remain respectful but conflict resolution is impossible under the circumstance.

What could you do now?

- Pray for your boss, asking God to help him to see the need for an amicable relationship. In addition, ask God to guide you in his appropriate timing, into employment where His name will be glorified through your conduct. Please note, wait on God's appropriate timing.

If you agree with this approach, then you would have demonstrated mastery in patience through your experiences. However, if as a part of your solution you believe you need to leave the job immediately as you are no longer able to cope with the conduct of your boss then it means you need to master the art of waiting on God patiently.

- Do not walk away from your job impulsively; it is time to reason. Do not allow impatience to meet patience as when this happens patience becomes impulsive. When you do not reason, you act without thinking. When you do not think through the steps leading to your actions, then you may take some actions that you may live to regret. Keep impatience away from patience at all times by reasoning.
- You will never know the benefits to be derived from your tests in patience if you constantly avert the process by being impatient.

James substantiates the importance of repeated tests in building patience:

My brethren count it all joy when you fall into various trials. Knowing that the testing of your faith produces patience. But let patience have its perfect work, that you may be perfect and complete, lacking nothing.

~James 1:2–4

Patience allows you to make decisions based on a cognitive process which enables you to weigh all your actions and their consequences. Impatience, on the other hand, is action without reasoning which usually results in regret.

Tests on patience will always be a part of life's experience. Your ability to cope will be dependent on how well you handle repeated tests. When you learn from previous experiences, when challenged again you will learn not to be impulsive but instead to wait on God. Pray, asking God to guide you daily, and be patient as you await His guidance.

– 12 –

Nature's Lesson on Patience, Humility and Pride and Valuable Lessons on Driving

God provides us with opportunities to learn patience in everything around us. The weather is an example of how we have to learn to accept what nature brings to us. It might be a wet day, yet you yearn for sunshine. Getting riled won't take away the rain drops and bring sunshine.

Fruits and other produce also teach us the importance of patience. If we pick the fruits from the tree before they are fit or ripened, they might make us ill or the taste might not be as appealing to our taste buds.

Pregnancy is another lesson on patience. Oh how we long to see if the baby looks like his or her mother, father, grandmother or grandfather, but we have to wait nine months to find out. God teaches us to wait on Him.

One of the most interesting lessons I have observed in nature on patience and humility is that of the lizard and the moth. Have you ever observed the process that leads to the conquest of a moth, which can fly, by a lizard on the wall that cannot? So you have not? Okay, let me tell you all about it.

The lizard is lying on the wall waiting to catch a few moths for dinner, knowing that it cannot fly. This may seem like an impossible task as the lizard is crawling and the moth is flying. The moth has every opportunity available to escape the mouth of the lizard. Does this escape always take place? No, Why? The reason is that Humility exercises Patience and then consumes Pride. When this happens, Pride falls and Humility rises as Patience is always a 'companion' of Humility. I hear you! You are wondering where this is going to end. . . . Having completed the lesson on Patience and Humility in previous chapters, let us relate what you have learnt to this chapter.

Be patient. . . . . I will get to the point.

In the example of the lizard and the moth we will have to identify the roles of Pride and Humility. As a hint, remember that Humility usually exercises Patience. I will describe my observation and allow you to determine Pride and Humility:

The lizard is lying on the wall. It appears as if it has accepted its limitation that it cannot fly. The lizard therefore uses the skills available to it which include crawling and raising its head. Every move it makes is calculated, exercising the degree of patience necessary to accomplish its task.

The moth, on the other hand, accepts that it can fly and does a good job demonstrating this (or is it showing off?). With observation, however, the moth's behavior seems to suggest a feeling of superiority over the lizard. Why? It flies close to the mouth of the lizard, hovering like an aeroplane over its head, demonstrating superiority as if saying, 'I can fly and you cannot, so watch me as I do this.'

LESSON ON PATIENCE, HUMILITY, PRIDE AND DRIVING

Have you determined who fits best the role of Pride, and Humility? Yes! So, I think we can agree that the moth represents Pride and the lizard Humility.

The lizard in its role as Humility is watching and waiting patiently for the opportune time. If it crawls or raises its head too early or too late then the lizard will not have a meal. So Humility (the lizard) has to use Patience to intercept Pride (moth) at the opportune moment, that is, when it catches the moth in its mouth. The moth is then destroyed. This is expressed Biblically:

Pride goes before destruction and a haughty spirit before a fall

~ Proverbs 16:18

The Little Oxford Dictionary and Thesaurus defines pride as an unduly high opinion of oneself. In this context the moth fits that definition.

God uses nature to teach us valuable lessons about how we can use pride to destroy our lives, and He also provides guidelines as to what is best for us:

Better to be of a humble spirit with the lowly, than to divide the spoil with the proud.

~ Proverbs 16:19

In addition, God informs us of the option that will ensure His guidance and blessings when we are obedient:

He who heeds the word wisely, will find good, and whoever trust in the Lord happy is he.

~ Proverbs 16:20

THE WORD

The principle of the destructive force of pride remains consistent for both the animal kingdom and for us as human beings. Let us ensure that if we find ourselves steering on the highway of Pride, a smooth road that most definitely will lead to destruction, let us get back on the 'Humility road'.

The 'humility road' is not smooth, but the frequent 'bumps' along the way serve as a reminder that we need to be cautious in our interactions with each other and in our thoughts, to avoid pride affecting our inter-personal relationships. On the other hand, the 'Pride road' is smooth and without bumps so there is no reminder or concern about the way God wants us to live.

Jesus wants us to benefit from eternal life and so He warns us to be careful of the way we live. In helping us to understand the impact of our choices, Jesus compares the example of the wide gate and the broad way with the narrow gate and the difficult way:

> *Enter by the narrow gate; for wide is the gate and broad is the way that leads to destruction and There are many who go in by it. Because narrow is the gate and difficult is the way which leads to life, and there are few who find it.*
>
> *~ Matthew 7: 13-14*

In our context today we can use the example of two drivers, one on a super highway, representing pride and the other on an unpaved road representing humility. The driver that is more likely to meet in a fatal accident would be the one on the super highway, the road that Jesus described as leading to destruction, pride. By a process of elimination the other driver on the unpaved road, the road that Jesus described as the

LESSON ON PATIENCE, HUMILITY, PRIDE AND DRIVING

difficult way, would represent humility and is less likely to meet in an accident.

Pride in our lives causes us to operate without spiritual guidelines and humility enables us to operate with spiritual guidelines provided by the Word of God. So, what lessons can we learn from the driver on the highway and the one on the unpaved road that will impact our lives positively? Let us explore together:

The highway provides a very smooth road that encourages speeding and therefore the driver does not think about the dangers of reckless driving. There are signs provided as guidelines for the speed at which the vehicle should travel. However, the speed at which the driver travels on this road is so fast that he is not able to see the signs providing words of caution and guidelines. Even if he sees them, he finds the road surface so irresistible, he cannot drive slowly and continues until he meets in an accident or is caught in a speed trap and has to pay the fine. That is the reality with pride; we get caught in our own trap as expressed previously:

Pride goes before destruction, and a haughty spirit before a fall.

~ Proverbs 16:18

What about the other driver on the unpaved road? That driver will not be able to speed as the road is so bumpy that all his efforts are concentrated on avoiding those large boulders or small craters in the road. The driver is able to see the speed limit signs clearly although it doesn't even affect him. The condition of the road is so bad that he is driving more slowly than the stipulated speed limit! (sigh!). All he can think about is the hope he has for a better life, one free from front-end repairs and new tyres for his motor vehicle. As he drives, he prays to God to help him achieve this objective. The driver on the super highway has no such concerns and in effect no prayers relating to his journey.

Highway driver, alias Pride, will certainly fall. Unpaved road driver, alias Humility, will be exalted one day as his eyes are on Jesus whom he is praying to for help to achieve a reduced car maintenance bill.

All of the above examples- the moth and the lizard, the superhighway and unpaved road drivers along with Jesus' example of the broad and the difficult way, reinforce the importance of humility and the need to avoid pride.

God provides us with so many lessons in nature to keep us humble. Start looking out for these and record what you learn from each experience. There are benefits to be gained when you are obedient and make the decision in your life to reduce pride and increase humility:

> *The fear of the Lord is the instruction of wisdom, and before honour is humility.*
>
> *~ Proverbs 15:33*

−13−

Discontentment

"I wish I had a new car" . . .

"I wish I had a bigger house so that I could invite all my friends over" . . .

"I wish I owned a yacht" . . .

Have you ever found yourself saying things like the statements above out loud, or thinking about them?

I believe your response is, yes. I think we are all guilty of making these statements or similar ones at some time or another. However, your responses to the questions below will determine if you are discontented:

- Are these statements as set out above or similar ones just made impulsively and then you settle back into life's routine without complaining?

Include your honest response in the space provided ....
....

- Do you dwell on your desires, hopes and dreams until it becomes difficult to accept your reality?

Include your honest response in the space provided................
....

THE WORD

When we are discontented we live in dream land wishing, hoping, moaning and groaning. That is a very miserable place to be. I will tell you right now that God hates when we get discontented. He loves us but when we are not satisfied and grateful with His provision then we are actually sending messages to God that we do not think He knows how to provide for our needs and we do not appreciate what He is doing. Are those the messages we really want to send to God, or is it that we have never thought about the real meaning behind our actions?

Today is the day for introspection:

- Am I happy with my life?

If your answer is no, is it because you are not accepting the conditions of your current life but instead, have fast forwarded the time machine to your fantasy life?

As human beings, we face conditions on a day to day basis that provide opportunities for us to learn and grow. When we understand that Adam's sin has resulted in our living in an imperfect world, then we will be able to accept our conditions as a part of life.

What is my point? There will be differences amongst us in so many things including our living standard, education, job opportunities and..

....

(Include differences you have observed in the space provided).

Now that we understand discontentment, let us learn more about how a discontented person behaves:

How does a discontented person impact the lives of others?
- By making others around them unhappy.

- By incessantly dwelling on what they do not have or on what they desire.

People have their own share of challenges/problems in this current life and to take on someone's moaning and groaning might be too much.

Instead of being discontented by dreaming or wishing, we should learn to enjoy and be grateful for what we currently have; in other words, be contented. Interestingly, what is the difference between the spelling of discontentment and contentment?

You are correct, the difference is, D I S. The acronym for D I S will help you see the need to be contented in this secular life:

DRIVE TO

INTERRUPT YOUR

SUCCESS

So, when you are discontented, you have used all your energies to interrupt or prevent your success.

- How do you interrupt your success?

You interrupt your success when you compare yourself with others and constantly bemoan your position in life. This means that you fail to use your energy to achieve your God given potential.

Look at this example:

- You are currently employed in an organization at the clerical level. However, you spend your time wishing you were the managing director. You have interrupted your success by losing focus.

What you should have been doing is to strive to be the best in your clerical role and improve your qualifications, which could lead to a promotion. Each promotion in your organization will improve your sense of worth and boost your self esteem.

Never forget that God has blessed us with talents and abilities and He wants us to use these to achieve our success. So, you need to avoid D I S, drive to interrupt your success, by hard work and determination which will increase your chance of success.

Today I want you to think about ways in which you have been discontented. Please state in the spaces provided your reasons for allowing discontentment to affect your life in the ways indicated or in others you choose to include:

- Comparing yourself with others.

....

- Constantly saying or thinking that God does not love you.

....

- Constantly saying or thinking that life is unfair to you.

....

- These things are happening to you because you are poor.

....

- You are disadvantaged because you do not have a high school or college education.

....

DISCONTENTMENT

- Others (list reasons not included above that may result in discontentment)

....
....

In order to avoid discontentment let us examine the life of a contented person:

- Accepts himself or herself as is. This includes acceptance of strengths, weaknesses, physical appearance, other. (Include in the space provided)..
- Is happy with his or her achievements.
- Does not allow himself or herself to become miserable by coveting what his or her neighbour has.
- Is happy for the success of others and saddened by their misfortunes as he or she sees no need for rivalry.
- Never compares himself or herself with others to highlight superiority or inferiority.

Having examined the life of a contented person, it appears that discontentment arises because persons do not accept themselves. Consequently, these persons strive to be like others whom they consider to be ideal.

Self acceptance therefore plays a significant role in contentment and includes acceptance of material acquisitions such as one's house, car and job without making a comparison with others who are deemed to be more successful.

Do you agree? If no, include your opinion in the space provided ....

In this materialistic world, people use their material acquisitions such as an expensive house, car or job promotion to seek validation from others. Include other ways in the space provided ....

Therefore, it becomes even more important to recognize the inherent danger in the quest for approval by others. What is my point? People will live beyond their means and plunge themselves into greater indebtedness in order to be accepted.

Be on your guard! Once you find yourself being covetous, greedy and desperate for acceptance, then these are the warning signals that you are becoming discontented. You will then be on the path to a miserable life whether you want to admit it or live in denial.

The Bible highlights the role that covetousness plays in leading us to discontentment:

> *Let your conduct be without covetousness; be content with such things as you have. For He Himself has said, "I will never leave you nor forsake you."*
>
> *~ Hebrews 13:5*

In our world today money is the medium of exchange used for material acquisition. Therefore, we have to be careful, as it can be a very destructive medium when used for selfish motives that cause us to be discontented with the amount we have, and results in our coveting others:

> *For the love of money is a root of all kinds of evil, for which some have strayed from the faith in their greediness, and pierced themselves through with many sorrows.*
>
> *~ 1 Timothy 6:10*

God has blessed His children and he wants us to use His blessings to His glory and for our good. However, if we become discontented and allow money, material gains or other things to control our lives we will destroy our relationship with each other and will retard our spiritual growth. God loves us and wants us to be contented so we can benefit from His blessings:

> *Now godliness with contentment is great gain.*
>
> *~ 1 Timothy 6: 6*

Continue reading to see the dangers in gaining riches without contentment:

> *But those who desire to be rich fall into temptation and a snare, and into many foolish and harmful lusts which drown men in destruction and perdition.*
>
> *~ 1 Timothy 6:9*

Okay, I believe some persons who are rich or who are striving to be rich will be murmuring about my argument, which appears to discourage riches in Christianity. The good news is that God is the one who is blessing you and He only wants to ensure that you use your riches in a Godly manner:

> *Command those who are rich in this present age not to be haughty, nor to trust in uncertain riches but in the living God who gives us richly things to enjoy. Let them do good, that they be rich in good works, ready to give willing to share.*
>
> *~ 1 Timothy 6: 17–18*

The rich become discontented because of their desire to become richer. Similarly, the poor become discontented because of their desire to acquire more in life. God uses His Word to remind us that once our basic needs are met we should be contented:

THE WORD

And having food and clothing, with these we shall be content.

~ 1 Timothy 6:8

For all of us, rich, middle-class and the poor, God's Word reminds us of the importance of being contented with our positions and possessions in life as we did not come into this world with material acquisition:

For we brought nothing into this world, and it is certain we can carry nothing out.

~ 1 Timothy 6:7

In life, our ultimate goal should be to ensure that we benefit from eternal life. This means, we should be contented. If we are discontented instead, this means there is some degree of covetousness in our lives as we look at others, or we feel disillusioned because our efforts are not matched by the rewards we think we deserve. We, however, need to remember that our lives on earth might be applauded by our fellow human beings but at the cost of our eternal life.

If we are successful here on earth and lose our eternal life, we have lost. However, we can have a win/win situation by adhering to God's Word and living a Godly life with contentment so we can benefit from eternal life. Our actions on earth are accumulating points towards eternal life or eternal damnation. If we are obedient to God on earth, our points would go towards eternal life:

Storing up for themselves a good foundation for the time to come, that they may lay hold on eternal life.

~ 1 Timothy 6:19

DISCONTENTMENT

When you start feeling covetous or are grumpy because you are discontented with how your life has turned out, please stop and express contentment in some of the ways listed below:

- Thank God for your life
- Thank God for His provisions
- Thank God for all the persons He has placed in your life
- Others .... (include other ways to be contented in the space provided).

There is no reason for you to believe that you are destined for failure as God wants you to prosper:

Beloved, I pray that you may prosper in all things and be in health, just as your soul prospers.

~3 John 1:2

As we strive to be obedient to God in these times, we need to acknowledge that we sometimes falter and sin. These weaknesses in our spiritual journey should cause us to feel discontented. The desire to please God should move us from a place of discontentment into a place of contentment through our actions so we can learn and grow spiritually.

How do we get to this place of contentment?

- Confess our sins and ask God for His forgiveness
- Read God's Word (The Holy Bible)
- Pray
- Fast
- Fellowship with other believers in church

- Others ....

(include your suggestions in the space provided).

Recall earlier in the chapter I stated that D I S prevents contentment in secular living, expressed as:

DRIVE TO

INTERRUPT YOUR

SUCCESS

However, in relation to your spiritual growth, D I S is expressed as:

DRIVE TO

INCREASE YOUR

SPIRITUAL GROWTH.

In our spiritual life, let our Drive to Increase Spiritual growth help us to strive for that place of contentment so that we can be 'shining' examples for Jesus.

In our secular life, let us also learn to be contented. If, however, there are things that you desire, you should set goals and ask God's guidance in helping you to achieve them.

Avoid discontentment and desist from comparing yourself with others. Be reminded that God wants you to prosper so seek His assistance and prosper according to His standard:

In all your ways acknowledge Him and He shall direct your paths.

~ Proverbs 3:6

– 14 –

Attitude

There is a popular expression that I learnt as a child that helped me to understand what attitude entails:

"It is not what happens but how you deal with what happens"

This statement taught me at an early age that regardless of the nature of the experience in life it is my response to it that will determine how well I cope.

Sometimes persons define attitude as one's outlook on life. How would you define attitude?

Include your definition in the space provided....................
....

I agree with the aforementioned definition of attitude. I believe it is important to highlight that one's outlook on life, or one's attitude to life can be either positive or negative and this will affect the way we relate to others in given circumstances. With a positive attitude, one is likely to see a challenge as an opportunity whereas the person with a negative attitude sees a challenge as a disaster.

One popular example of the impact of positive attitude led to the success of the Bata Shoes Company in Africa, over other shoes company from England. Marketing representatives from the other shoes manufacturing companies in England concluded that there was no market for shoes in Africa, as the people there did not wear them. On the other hand, the Bata Shoe Company representative acknowledged the fact that no one in Africa wore shoes but saw this as an ideal opportunity for a huge market for their product.

The African market for the Bata Shoe Company was very successful and as a result Bata shoes are described as the shoes of Africa. The success of the Bata Shoe Company confirms that our attitude can determine our success or failure.

Attitude affects every aspect of our lives and we need to be aware of this so that we can develop a thought pattern that leads to productive rather than destructive thoughts and actions.

Let us examine our attitude towards getting up out of bed in the morning as this helps to determine our actions for the day.

If you are in a bad mood and do not feel like getting up and going to work or school or doing any other activity you had previously planned, you would have set the pace for your mood for the day. Usually, your attitude towards your day will be reflected in your response to others.

One popular response by others to a negative attitude from an individual early in the morning is:

"It appears as if you got up on the wrong side of the bed this morning."

This statement substantiates the point that one's attitude upon getting out of bed in the morning sets the pace for the rest of the day.

- It is natural for us to experience mood swings which include feeling happy, sad, grumpy and others .... (Include your feelings in the space provided).

- When we are unhappy we usually penalize the world by being curt, sarcastic, unkind, others.................................... (Include ways in which you penalize others in the space provided).

I will make my confession, 'I too am guilty of taking out my mood swings on the first 'victim' that crosses my path in the mornings when I am in a bad mood.'

However, I am learning (please note, it is a continuous process) to control my mood swings.

Our thought process affects our attitude and ultimately our behaviour. Do you agree? This means that our mood swings would therefore be as a result of our thought process, that is, how we mentally interpret the experience or circumstance that impacts our lives. Our thoughts and the way we relate to others are usually determined by a number of factors which include socialization and our responses from previous experiences. Let me use an example of each:

Socialization

An employer from a wealthy family has been socialized to treat the poor as inferior. In interacting with a poor employee this could be reflected in how he or she communicates disrespectfully with that employee. On the other hand, the poor person could have been socialized to be defensive, vindictive or patronizing towards the rich. The poor person's attitude could be reflected in words or action when communicating with the rich employer.

Include your example on socialization in the space provided

....

....

Previous Experience

You have previously been denied your vacation leave in favour of another employee, who you were informed had an emergency and needed leave for the same period you had applied for.

- You have made recent plans to travel and are really looking forward to getting your current leave application approved. Your supervisor has sent you an email to meet with her to discuss your leave application. You enter the meeting with a defensive attitude based on your disappointment with the outcome of your previous leave application. You are angry.

- However, the meeting with your supervisor was favourable. All she wanted to do was to congratulate you on your improved performance and to apologize for not approving your previous leave application due to your co-worker's need for emergency leave at the time.

These examples demonstrate the impact of our thought process on our behaviour. We should also bear in mind that God does not expect us to discriminate against each other as highlighted in the example on socialization. We are all children of God and He has a purpose for us just as we are. Class, race, wealth, poverty, physique, ... (Include other examples in the space provided) should not be used as weapons of 'attitude' resulting in discrimination in our interaction with others.

In addition, we need to remember that our values,..............
....
(Include examples of values in the space provide) also help to determine our attitude.

Attitude is expressed not only verbally but also non-verbally in our facial expressions and body language.

A popular expression used for attitude that is expressed through our facial expression or body language is:

"You are giving me an attitude."

Remember, a positive attitude always aids in improving interpersonal relationships. The problem is our negative attitude.

I will share with you an approach that will help to convert your negative attitude, whether as a result of socialization, previous experience, mood swings or otherwise, to a more positive attitude that will make others feel more comfortable in your presence.

Converting Negative Attitude to Positive Attitude

Questions you need to ask yourself that will confirm your negative attitude. Your honest responses to the questions below will determine whether you have a bad attitude:

- How do I reflect a bad attitude? Is it my tone, words, actions?

....
....

- How does my negative attitude affect others? Do they ignore, avoid or abuse me?

....
....

- Do I enjoy amicable relationships with my negative attitude?

....
....

- What can I do to ensure that I adapt a more positive attitude to life?

....
....

The Approach

I have created the PQRS approach, an acronym to help you exhibit a more positive attitude:

PROBLEMS ARISE

QUESTIONS ARE NEEDED

RESPONSES TO THESE PROVIDE

SOLUTION

Your negative attitude is usually triggered by some problem(s) that you are experiencing or anticipate you will experience. There are some persons who believe that there will always be problems in their lives and if these are not occurring they are anticipated. Such a person is usually referred to as a prophet or prophetess of gloom and doom. Do you anticipate problems?

If yes, include your reasons in the space provided ....
....

ATTITUDE

If you welcome thoughts about your problems without thinking about solutions then you will embrace and reflect a negative attitude. This is something you should never do. Instead, having recognized the Problem with your attitude you need to ask yourself some Questions:

How am I feeling right now?

State your feelings in the space provided............................
....

If your feelings are negative (miserable, grumpy . . .) your next question would be:

- How does my mood affect others?

   Include your response in the space provided.......................
....

Your responses to the questions above should help you see the need to make changes in your attitude.

- How do I adjust my mental state?

Your response to be included in the space provided below to this final question will provide the solutions to a change in your attitude from negative to positive. This will result in improved interpersonal relationship with others....................
....

Consider the following suggestions to assist with your solution:

- You first need to accept that there is a genuine problem and believe that you will overcome as Jesus promised:

   These things I have spoken to you, that in Me you may have Peace. In the world you will have tribulation; but be of good cheer, I have overcome the world.

   ~ John 16:33

THE WORD

Jesus said it, and it is so. Life will be fraught with problems but you are never alone. For every problem you experience and feel all alone in, there are many others who have had a similar experience, and God's Word confirms this:

> *No temptation has overtaken you except such as is common to man; but God is faithful, who will not allow you to be tempted beyond what you are able, but with the temptation will also make the way of escape, that you may be able to bear it.*
>
> ~ *1 Corinthians 10:13*

God's Word reassures us that with our problems there will be solutions.

Look back on chapter 6, "Overcoming Challenges", to help you identify the resources that you have readily available to help with solving your problems.

If the problem is imagined, recognize that you are afraid of what might happen and your fear has driven you to worry unnecessarily. Unfortunately, in many instances the fear becomes the problem in our lives as we become stressed and ruin our health over things that will not happen.

Learn to trust Jesus and ask for His help with your fears:

> *Casting all your care upon Him, for He cares for you.*
>
> ~ *1 Peter 5:7*

In addition, read your Bible daily and believe God's Word:

> *For God has not given us a spirit of fear, but of power and of love and of a sound mind.*
>
> ~ *Timothy 1:7*

God wants us to share with each other our problems and fears (both real and imagined) and so He encourages us in His Word:

Bear one another's burdens, and so fulfill the law of Christ.

~ Galatians 6: 2

It is sometimes difficult for us to trust others enough to share our problems, as we fear being exposed. We do not want to know that our problems are being discussed. Ask God to guide you to someone in your church or to a friend who is compassionate and confidential. Solving problems takes time and so, while we wait, we might not be as cheerful to others as we usually are. In order not to destroy our relationships with a negative attitude, be polite and tell those you interact with that your changed mood has to do with your personal issues and ask for their understanding.

Practice the PQRS Method to help you conquer your negative attitude, improve your interpersonal relationship with others and enjoy a healthier lifestyle.

For those persons who usually demonstrate a positive attitude, continue to do so and share your approach with others. This will enable more persons to lead healthier and happier lives.

Of course, God always has the final words for us so when we are tempted to focus on the problems/negatives, remember to use His Word as our guide:

Finally, brethren, whatever things are true, whatever things are noble, whatever things are just, whatever things are pure, whatever things are lovely, whatever things are of good report, if there is any virtue and if there is anything praiseworthy, meditate on these things.

~ Philippians 4:8

– 15 –

Unforgiveness

Forgiveness is very important in order to maintain our relationship with others after they have hurt us. As human beings we often hurt others intentionally or unintentionally which may cause physical or emotional suffering. From time to time persons become angry with others, some may feel betrayed or find it difficult to continue in the relationship as bitterness reigns. This unwillingness to forgive has greater repercussions for the persons who are hurt, the offended, than for the ones who hurt us, the offenders.

Our natural tendency as human beings is to be vindictive so we ensure that we hurt those who have hurt us. We sometimes go to the extreme in our acts of vindictiveness which at times result in fatal endings to relationships, reprisal killings, verbal and physical abuse.

There are numerous health risks that are involved when you become embittered because of unforgiveness. So you need to ask yourselves the question: Is it worth it to destroy my health and happiness simply because I refuse to forgive another person?

NO! It can never be worth it. While it is always easy for us to rehearse our hurt, we need to understand that in doing so it is more likely to cause greater pain to us than if we let go of it. I will use the analogy of getting a wound to demonstrate the impact of unforgiveness in our lives:

You accidentally cut yourself while cooking. The pain from the wound is unbearable. Please tell me which of the two things stated below would aid in the healing process:

- Apply treatment to the wound so that it will heal.
- Sit and look at the wound and rehearse the incident that caused the wound.

Yes! Bullet one, applying treatment to the wound would be the best option to aid in the healing process.

To translate the principle with the wound into your everyday relationship with others, it would be more beneficial to forgive (to treat the wound) than to remain angry and vindictive (keep the wound untreated).

Let us go back to the story of how to treat the wound:

- The doctor would need the relevant information as to how you were wounded to help with the treatment process.

Let us assume that the knife that caused the wound was old and rusty. This means that a tetanus injection might be necessary. Am I correct? While, I am not a medical doctor I hope the example is meaningful. The point is that once the relevant information is given to the doctor, treatment would then be prescribed accordingly and it would not be necessary to repeat the information about how you were wounded (with the knife).

- The next step would be to apply the medication that would eventually aid in the healing of the wound.

Is there a difference in the way we deal with the wound from a cut from a knife as opposed to the pain we feel when someone has hurt us?

As human beings when we are hurt by others we like to vent, as this is cathartic. If, however, we keep rehearsing the incident, we move from catharsis to intensifying our pain. In many instances, what we do is talk to as many persons repeatedly who are willing to entertain our story.

Like the wound, talking will not result in healing or forgiveness. As a matter of fact, talking is likely to intensify your anger and increase your bitterness as you repeat the experience of your past hurt.

With every repetition you are likely to become more vindictive by just wanting to hurt the other person.

Have you ever experienced that feeling, or have persons share with you their pain of being hurt and their desire to be vindictive to those who have hurt them?

Include your response in the space provided......................
....

Vindictiveness makes us less friendly, more hostile and unhappy.

Before examining the steps in healing the wound of 'unforgiveness' let us look at what the healing process entails in our analogy with the wound. The wound resulting from the cut has to be treated.

The need to treat the wound means that there is an actual injury. Agree? There would be a visible cut and this means that some object caused your injury. Treatment of the wound is therefore an acknowledgement or acceptance that the knife had cut you. I know so far it might be difficult to follow my line of argument, just relax and be patient the puzzle will be completed in time.

Let us now examine the healing process with 'unforgiveness':

- The person who is struggling with unforgiveness has to accept that he or she has been hurt by someone. This is necessary as, in order for healing to take place, the pain or hurt has to be first acknowledged. Please note, acknowledgement of the pain is not achieved when the experience is reiterated to several persons. A mere mental reflection of the incident or sharing the experience with a trusted friend or professional is adequate.

Persons who hurt others might not consider their actions as causing pain. They might not even care about the feelings of the persons they hurt or they might be living in denial thereby avoiding the need to acknowledge that they have hurt others.

To be hurt and not to be acknowledged by the offender could be seen by some persons as a justified reason to be angry and unforgiving. Bear in mind when we become unforgiving, we become like the untreated wound that gets infected. In like manner, you could endanger your own health by your actions, which could lead to high blood pressure, heart disease or other illnesses (Yes! 'unforgiveness' can destroy you physically).

What are some of the other ways unforgiveness can affect you?

- You could find yourself isolated by others because you have become so miserable in your 'unforgiving state.'

- Persons get tired of hearing your 'sad' story about the ones who have hurt you. In many instances, these persons have encouraged you to forgive but you have not accepted their suggestions.

I do agree that people will empathize with you when you are hurt. However, if your story is constantly rehearsed, people will sometimes doubt its authenticity or view you as an attention seeker.

So far, I have discussed with you the consequences of unforgiveness which include health risks and poor interpersonal relationships with others. Let us now look at the benefits relating to forgiveness.

Let us formulate a definition for forgiveness. Forgiveness is a conscious effort to willingly pardon another person for an act of wrongdoing. In effect you choose to avoid being vindictive towards persons who have hurt you. Please note the use of the word willingly, which means, an exercise of your freewill. You should not be coerced into forgiving or hope that the offender will feel remorse.

Furthermore, you should not give the impression that you are a forgiving person when you know genuinely that this is not so. If you choose to do so, it could come back to haunt you in ways that you might live to regret. Think seriously about it! Have you ever pretended to forgive someone and then find yourself getting angry at that person when anger was not justified as a response? Yes? All that happened was that you harboured feelings of unforgiveness about a past incident and it resurfaced when you least expected. Let us examine our motive as we strive to forgive each other and ensure that we are genuine in what we do.

The conversation with Jesus and Peter on forgiveness shows that forgiveness is a personal effort which is not dependent on a response from the one causing the hurt:

> *Then Peter came to Him and said, "Lord, how often shall my brother sin against me, and I forgive him? Up to seven times?" Jesus said to him, "I do not say to you, up to seven times, but up to seventy times seven.*
>
> *~ Matthew 18:21-22*

Interestingly, Peter was prepared to forgive seven times but Jesus told Peter it was seventy times seven.

I am not a mathematics expert so I will leave you to calculate the number of times Jesus expects us to forgive. What is important is that Jesus encourages us to be liberal with forgiveness.

It is important at this juncture to highlight that forgiveness and reconciliation are not the same. Reconciliation, unlike forgiveness, requires both the person hurting and the person causing the hurt to work together to resolve the issue which should culminate in a more amicable relationship. Verbal communication would provide an opportunity for both parties to express their feelings and their expectations of each other.

Never forget that some persons might not want to reconcile, as usually this entails a promise not to hurt each other and also entails the need to forgive. We need to remember that as human beings God has given us free will which enables us to choose.

In light of this you cannot force your offenders to reconcile with you if they are not interested in having a relationship. You, on the other hand, might want to be reconciled with your offender and find the person's refusal unfair.

The mistake you should never make is to accept a person's

refusal to reconcile with you as sending a message that you are not someone of worth. Some persons, after communicating to their offender their willingness to forgive and their desire to be reconciled, experience a shattered sense of self worth because of the person's body language and verbal response including:

- 'I do not care'
- 'You do not mean anything to me.'
- 'You are history now.'
- Others ....
  (include other examples in the space provided).

Similarly, persons who are hurt might not want to be reconciled with the persons who have hurt them.

God wants His children to live in harmony and He wants us to worship Him knowing that all our attempts at reconciliation have been made before we come to His altar (highlighted in chapter 8):

> *Therefore, if you bring your gift to the altar, and there remember that your brother has something against you. Leave your gift there before the altar, and go your way. First be reconciled to your brother, and then come and offer your gift.*
>
> *~ Matthew 5: 23-24*

Jesus recognizes that there are times when others will be offended by our actions even though we ourselves are not malicious towards them. Our Prince of Peace, Jesus, encourages us to reconcile with our fellow brothers and sisters before offering our gifts to Him at the altar.

Is there someone today that you believe is displeased with you? If yes, stop reading right now and reconcile, as Jesus requires of us. Once you have reconciled or have at least done your best at attempting to reconcile, continue your reading.

I know it is not easy to reconcile with some persons based on their personality (aggressive, malicious............................
....
(include other examples in the space provided).

Jesus knows us and has set a criteria for us to deal with our attempts at reconciliation:

Moreover, if your brother sins against you, go and tell him his fault between you and him alone. If he hears you, you have gained your brother. But if he will not hear, take with you one or two more, that by the mouth of two or three witnesses every word may be established. And if he refuses to hear them, tell it to the church. But if he refuses even to hear the church, let him be to you like a heathen and a tax collector.

~ Matthew 18: 15-17

What is important is that God wants us to understand that His objective is for us to live harmoniously and where reconciliation is needed this should be done in obedience to God. What is important is to make a genuine effort to reconcile with your offender. Whether you succeed or fail at reconciliation, remember that God expects you to forgive the other person.

Forgiveness on your part should not be used as a bargaining tool in an effort to get the other person to be reconciled to you, but instead it should serve as a reminder that God will only forgive you when you forgive others:

THE WORD

For if you forgive men their trespasses, your heavenly Father will also forgive you. But if you do not forgive men their trespasses, neither will your Father forgive your trespasses.

~ *Matthew 6:14-15*

To reinforce the importance of forgiveness in our lives Jesus reminds us that if we are praying and are guilty of 'unforgiveness' we need to forgive:

And whenever you stand praying, if you have anything against anyone, forgive him, that your Father In heaven may also forgive you your trespasses.

~ *Mark 11:25*

God's lessons to us on forgiveness and reconciliation are clear.

In summary, God says if you are guilty of having something against someone you should forgive that person. On the other hand, reconcile where you believe another person has something against you. Reconciliation involves dialogue, and this gives you both the opportunity to express your feelings and clear up any misunderstanding.

What an opportunity! Are you ready to forgive? If you are not, this is what you are depriving yourself of:

- Peace

- The avoidance of health risks including high blood pressure, stress ....

(Include others in the space provided).

- The Spiritual benefit of being forgiven by God as if we are not, our hope of eternal life is lost. In summary, this means, no forgiveness, no heaven.

I know we will all strive to forgive others starting now.

I will do a quick review on the steps to forgiveness using the principles from the illustration of the wound:

Step 1

- Look at your wound.

What are you feeling?
Is it physical, emotional or verbal pain?
Step 1 helps you to identify the ways in which you have been hurt by your offender resulting in 'unforgiveness'.

Step 2

- Recall the person who hurt you.

Who caused your wound?
Name the person
This step helps you to accept that you have been hurt by that person.

Acceptance does not mean that you are endorsing what was done to you as being right. You are only acknowledging that you have been hurt by that person and that the pain has led you or is leading you to a place of 'unforgiveness'.

Step 3

- Applying medication to the wound.

In other words, what do I need to do to forgive my offender? Some of the things include:

- Praying and asking God to help you to forgive your offender and then release the pain.

- Avoid repeating the incident to others (this is after speaking about it with a trusted friend).

- Where possible, if the offender expresses genuine remorse and is willing to communicate with you, then do so. Let the person know that you have forgiven him or her.
- If the offender refuses to speak with you and has no remorse about his or her action, then all you can do is forgive and leave everything to God.

This step helps you to achieve the will of God in avoiding bitterness by forgiving.

Step 4

- Watch the wound heal.

How do you know when the wound is healing?

- When you are more peaceful
- Less embittered, less stressed and more sociable.

Step 4 helps you to avoid illnesses related to 'unforgiveness'.

Step 5

- Look out for re-infection?

What is likely to cause this?
Some of the things include:

- Not forgiving your offender genuinely.
- Refusal of the offender to, reconcile or apologize.
- Rehearsing the incident to others and thereby intensifying your pain and anger.
- Being vindictive to your offender.

This step provides warning signals to remind you that you are destroying your life physically and spiritually.

Step 6

- How do you treat a re-infection?

With Spiritual Antibiotics which is:

- Prayer – asking God to forgive you and to help you to forgive the offender.

- Reading your Bible and applying God's criteria for forgiveness and reconciliation in Matthew 6: 14-15 and Mark 11: 25.

Step 7

- How do you know when your re-infection is healing?

When you are:

- Happier, less stressed and see other visible signs as set out in Step 4.

Use these steps as a guide as you battle with forgiving others. Remember God's Word as He provides you with the strength to make the change from 'unforgiveness' to forgiveness:

I can do all things through Christ who strengthens me.

~ Philippians 4:13

– 16 –

Thanksgiving

I want to ask you one question but before I do, I want you to promise me that your response will be sincere. I know I won't hear it but let your conscience be your guide. Have you ever had an experience where you did a good deed for someone and that person was ungrateful?

If your answer is yes to the above question, how did that person's ingratitude make you feel?

Include your response in the space provided......................
....

If your answer to the question is no, I assume that you have done acts of good deed but have never encountered ingratitude by any of the recipients of your kind acts. My question to you then is, how do you think you would feel if you had such an experience?

Include your response in the space provided ....
....

I anticipate your question for me, how do I react when faced with ingratitude? Honestly, I am usually annoyed. One such instance is driving, when I allow someone coming on to the main road ahead of me in traffic. Realistically, slowing to allow a person to come out ahead of another in traffic has its fair share of potential mishaps. Usually, the driver behind me is coming down at full speed despite my brake lights which are sending a message to that person to follow suit and slow down. In order to avoid collusion with my rear bumper I usually have to swerve at an angle relying totally on God's miracle working power to avert an accident. Thank you God!

Can you imagine all that drama and trauma to allow someone ahead of you in traffic? Then the person comes out, holds his or her head high with dignity and drives without honking the horn as a sign of gratitude. I get really annoyed! What about you?

State your experience in the space provided ....
....

I sometimes reflect on how God is merciful in allowing the person behind me to apply his or her brake a fraction of an inch from my rear bumper and how He guided me to swerve at the right time. Yet this driver that I allowed ahead of me did not say thanks!

Of course we are all humans and such minuscule acts of generosity can be annoying when not acknowledged by the recipient. Note I said minuscule acts of generosity (so small that we should not even make a fuss if gratitude is not expressed to us). Can you imagine how God feels? He must be so hurt at our ingratitude.

Look at all the things God has done for us and continues to do. Remember we would not be here if God did not give us life. God has provided for us in so many ways each day of our lives. So, we should give thanks for all God has done, is doing and will continue to do for us:

THE WORD

- Thank you, God, for life and for waking us up each day.
- Thank you, God, for oxygen, the air we breathe to live.
- Thank you, God, for the way you've made our bodies as David reminds us:

I will praise You, for I am fearfully and wonderfully made; marvelous are your works, and that my soul knows very well.

~ Psalm 139-14

I would not have enough paper and ink to record all of God's goodness. I have listed a few so you can complete your long list in your own time.

I assure you, if you were to record all your blessings it will take your life-time to complete. Yes, it will. Remember we receive God's goodness every day of our lives. God is awesome! This gives us one more reason to say, 'Thank you, God.'

Can you imagine? God loves us so much that He made us in His image. We, however, had to destroy our relationship with God through the disobedience of Adam and Eve. This resulted in our separation from God and the ensuing struggles in our lives. God however, sent His only Son, Jesus Christ to die on a cross bearing the shame so we can have the opportunity to enjoy eternal life with them. Isn't this exciting? We now have more reasons to express our gratitude:

Thank you, God, for eternal life. We will never die again after the first death at the end of our mortal lives. Please do not forget that you will have to face judgement for the way you lived your life on earth. If your acts are pleasing to God you will enjoy eternal life. If they are not, you will experience eternal damnation, fire and brimstone.

THANKSGIVING

On judgement day you cannot tell God that you were not aware of what He expected of you. Why? God's Word details everything He expects of us so start reading now, before it is too late!

We have examined some of the reasons for giving thanks to God. I need your response to the questions below after you have done some introspection on your reasons for thanksgiving:

What is your motive for giving thanks?..............................
....

Do you believe that people should give thanks to God with the expectation that their gratitude will result in greater blessings from God?

Your response...

Thanksgiving is a way of demonstrating that we love and appreciate God's goodness and this should be done sincerely. It is also an indication of our faith in God when we face trials and all seems impossible. In these periods of trials we can confidently hold on to the fact that God never fails as He is faithful and always keeps His promise. Despite our circumstances we are assured that He is working His purpose out. We know confidently that we are being taken care of and that provides adequate reasons to be thankful:

In everything give thanks for this is the will of God in Christ Jesus for you.
~ I Thessalonians 5:18

Thanksgiving entails communicating with God as He expects us to in the many ways He has provided. This includes praying, reading His Word, songs, playing musical instruments, dancing and sharing your testimonies.

The world abounds with God's goodness to us through

creation. I highlight this as many persons believe that thanksgiving relates to only the things we receive in our lives from God. Oh no! Thanksgiving is our way of showing our appreciation to God for who He is as our Heavenly Father, Creator of the universe, our Guide, Provider, Redeemer, Judge and..

....

(Include others in the space provided).

We should no longer need any reminder to give thanks to God as our very existence on this beautiful planet, earth, provides adequate reasons for gratitude. You should be thrilled to give thanks every day of your life to God who is worthy to be praised.

Live with an attitude of gratitude and remember God inhabits the praise of His people. God is pleased when we give thanks:

> *It is good to give thanks to the Lord, and to sing praises to Your name, O Most High; To declare Your loving kindness in the morning, and your faithfulness every night, On an instrument of ten strings, on the lute, and on the harp, with harmonious sound, For, You, Lord have made me glad through Your work; I will triumph in the works of Your hand.*
>
> ***~ Psalm 92:1–4***

– 17 –

Giving

In a period of recession such as we are now living in, most persons find it difficult to be generous.

Persons fear that they will be made redundant from their jobs and in an effort to ensure that they will always have a reserve to cope with emergencies, they withhold their scarce resources. Giving during periods of crisis is usually done grudgingly or not at all as our natural response would be for self preservation.

Let us look at the conversation between Elijah and the widow from Zarephath who God had provided to feed Elijah during the period of drought. On arrival in Zarephath Elijah asked her for a drink of water (Read 1 Kings chapter 17 for the full account):

> *And as she was going to get it, he called her and said, "Please bring me a morsel of bread in your hand." So she said, "As the Lord your God lives, I do not have bread, only a handful of flour in a bin, and a little oil in a jar; and see, I am gathering a couple of sticks that I may go in and prepare it for myself and my son, that we may eat it and die."*
>
> ~1 Kings 17: 11–12

THE WORD

The widow's response is similar to our behavior as human beings in crisis. We can then conclude that human behaviour in a crisis is consistent regardless of the era in which we live when faced with limited resources. There will always be the exception, persons who can afford to give but who are not generous by nature.

Let's go back to the story of the widow, she was faced with an uncertain future, a drought with limited food supply and so giving for her wasn't a priority. Her priority was to bake two cakes one for her son and one for herself and they would both eat them then die. Despite her uncertain future, Elijah's words brought hope:

> *And Elijah said to her, "Do not fear; go and do as you have said, but make me a small cake from it first, and bring it to me; and afterwards make some for yourself and your son. "For thus says the lord God of Israel: 'The bin of flour shall not be used up, nor shall the jar of oil run dry, until the day the Lord sends rain on the earth.'"*
>
> ~ 1 Kings 17: 13-14

Elijah's command, with the assurance from God that she would always have oil and meal if she baked a cake for him first, prompted her to do as he had suggested. This was done because she believed:

> *So she went away and did according to the word of Elijah; and she and he and her house-hold ate for many days.*
>
> ~ I Kings 17:15

If she had doubted Elijah she would have settled for one meal only and then died but she believed and her food supply was not depleted:

The bin of flour was not used up, nor did the jar of oil run dry, according to the word of the Lord which He spoke by Elijah.

~ I Kings 17:16

What would you have done if, you were asked to give under circumstances as trying as this widow was experiencing?

Remember, this woman was having an encounter with Elijah for the first time. She didn't have an opportunity to build a relationship with him. She was willing, however, in light of her circumstances, to have faith and believe.

The experience of this widow provides an opportunity for us to think about our own lives and how we react to giving when faced with an uncertain future.

If this woman was able to have faith in a complete stranger in times of crisis, shouldn't we find it easier to give to a God who never fails?

We know that God loves us, He wants the best for us and He will never fail us. The experience with the widow from Zarephath sets the stage for us to now look at tithing to God.

TITHING

The first question you might need an answer to is: what is tithing?

Tithing is the giving of one tenth of your earnings to God. Emphasis is placed on the first ten percent. If you are employed the amount for your tithes should be calculated based on your gross earnings, that is, before statutory and all other deductions including mortgage, car loans, furniture loans, school fees and..

....

(list your expenses in the space provided).

If you are self employed then the principle remains the same, your tithe should be calculated based on your gross income and not net income as illustrated below:

The Farmer

Each time the farmer reaps and sells his or her produce, one-tenth of the gross earnings should be given as his or her tithes weekly, monthly or based on how sales are made.

Other Persons

Tithe would be calculated and paid based on how the gross income is earned whether weekly, monthly or otherwise. In this category would be all persons who are not employed by an organization or an individual and are deemed by law to be accountable for all statutory deductions as well as other expenses relating to their income and include:

- Doctors and, lawyers in private practice
- Skilled, semi-skilled and unskilled workers
- Include the nature of your self-employment in the space provided..

....

Now that you understand how to calculate your tithes, your comment might include:

- God doesn't need my earnings
- I have more expenses than my current earnings
- God already owns everything
- Include other responses in the space provide ....

....

All of the above are comments we are likely to make with regards to our tithe. However, God's Word states:

If I were hungry, I would not tell you; for the world is Mine, and all its fullness.

~ Psalm 50:12

God doesn't need our tithes, but His work uses it for His Glory. Tithes are used for paying the ministers, all the church ministries that will help to spread the gospel, aiding the poor members in the church, outreach - programmes in the communities and to aid others who might request help from the church.

However, if you choose not to give, God will still have persons who are faithful and obedient to him. God's power can bring into being anything he is desirous of achieving.

I am going to digress to prove my point. Do you remember how God asked Abraham to sacrifice his only son? I am sure you will recall Abraham's willingness to kill his only son. In effect, giving him back to God:

And Abraham stretched out his hand and took the knife to slay his son. But the Angel of the Lord called to him from heaven and said, "Abraham, Abraham! So he said, "Here I am". And he said, "Do not lay your hand on the lad, or do anything to him; for now I know that you fear God, since you have not withheld your son, your only son, from Me."

~ Genesis 22: 10-12

God told Abraham that he had demonstrated faithfulness by his willingness to offer his son as a sacrifice.

With God we never lose, Abraham was willing to give his

son to God for a burnt offering and God gave to Abraham a ram to be used instead:

> *Then Abraham lifted his eyes and looked, and there behind him was a ram caught in a thicket by its horns. So Abraham went and took the ram, and offered it up for a burnt offering instead of his son.*
>
> *~ Genesis 22:13*

Would you give back your only child to God if He asked you? What if God asked you to give Him back your mansion, ...

(Include your vehicle in the space provided) or other status symbols in the society, would you?

Think about these questions . . .

Remember all that you own and will ever own are gifts from God. You might say you have worked hard for these things. You need to face the reality, without God's blessings you would not have been able to achieve these things.

As highlighted previously, God didn't allow Abraham to kill his only son although a sacrifice was needed. What did God do for Abraham? He provided a ram which was caught in the thicket to be used for the sacrifice. You should recall that earlier I mentioned if you do not give, God still has persons who are willing to give. These persons will learn to be sacrificial and disciplined, valuable lessons in character building. Do you really want to miss this opportunity?

God is not asking you for your house, car or status in society as previously mentioned. All that God is asking you for is one-tenth of your gross income. Would you agree that God is reasonable and merciful in what he expects from us? God could have asked for fifty-percent. Would you prefer that?

Let us read the benefits we will receive when we tithe:

Bring all the tithes into the storehouse, that there may be food in My house, and try Me now in this, says the Lord of hosts. If I will not open for you the windows of heaven and pour out for you such blessing that there will not be room enough to receive it.

~ *Malachi 3:10*

How much does God expect from us when we give our tithes?

As already stated, one tenth of our gross earnings and not less. Remember when God gives us a command, if we obey we benefit and if we don't it is our loss. Our response to God's command is an indication of how we feel about God. When we tithe, this indicates our obedience to God as we do His command.

As we give, we build our faith and trust in God knowing that He will take care of us.

We will not begin tithing genuinely unless we believe God's Word; then as we are obedient to Him relationship building takes place during tithing.

The chapters on believing, faith and relationship building are vital in helping us to understand the importance of tithing.

God's Word provides evidence of His love for us, that He is working on our behalf and He expects us to be obedient to Him. When you withhold from God by not tithing, in effect, you withhold from yourself (Do you want to deprive yourself of God's blessings?).

Let's go through the steps in tithing to ensure that you have cemented what God expects from you:

THE WORD

Step 1

Set aside your first fruits, before you start spending, and give it in God's house. First fruits mean the first ten per cent, from your gross earnings before all statutory and other deductions. In a world where there is focus on materialism and self centeredness receiving is more practised than giving. In obedience to God, however, do as He tells you to do. Giving prevents us from being selfish as we learn to think how others will benefit from our tithes as we share God's blessings.

Use the example of the widow from Zarephath as a reminder of the importance of giving. Remember, she gave the first cake she baked to Elijah and then baked for her son and herself.

This widow's action demonstrated the principle associated with tithing when she believed, had faith and was obedient to God through Elijah's command to her.

You will recall that Elijah told the widow that she would always have meal and oil if she baked the first cake and gave it to him. However, the power to increase the meal and oil came from God. As human beings we need to always accept the fact that ultimately it is God's power that performs miracles. Being aware of this fact prevents us from ascribing to our fellow human beings the power and the praise that belongs to God.

In the process of tithing, there are persons who will tell you the many ways in which you will be blessed when you tithe. If this happens, it did because God allowed it and not because of what these persons have said. Let me reiterate, God is the only one who has the power to bless us, so do not be fooled into believing otherwise.

Step 2

Give your tithes willingly, not grudgingly. Remember God loves a cheerful giver:

> *But this I say: He who sows sparingly will also reap sparingly, and he who sows bountifully will also reap bountifully. So let each one give as he purposes in his heart, not grudgingly or of necessity; for God loves a cheerful giver.*
>
> *~ 2 Corinthians 9:6-7*

Step 3

Give your tithes with an attitude of gratitude and not an attitude of expectancy:

> *I have shown you in every way, by laboring like this, that you must support the weak. And remember the words of the Lord Jesus, that He said, 'It is more blessed to give than to receive.'*
>
> *~ Acts 20:35*

God wants us to be grateful and to give thanks to Him for His provisions. If He did not bless us in the first place we would not have anything to give. You need to tell God that you appreciate the source of income that he has provided for you whether as an employed or self employed individual.

Giving with an attitude of expectancy from God defeats the objective in tithing. Tithing is one of the many ways in which we demonstrate our love for God. When we give with an attitude of expectancy it becomes a bargaining tool where we expect God to give us cash or kind in exchange for our tithes.

I know that in giving to each other we sometimes apply a similar principle, bargaining, giving with an attitude of expectancy.

The examples below will serve as a reminder of some of the things we might be guilty of in giving to each other:

- The Christmas gift that you gave hoping that when it was received by that person, he or she would give you something just as expensive or even more expensive. Do you agree?
- Refusal to buy a gift for someone until you receive one from that person so that you can determine how much you should spend. Has this ever happened to you?

I have deviated from tithing to gift giving so that as you think about your motive for giving to each other this will help you to recall times when your sole reason for tithing was a selfish motive, to get from God things you desired. List below times when your sole motive for tithing was to receive from God and ask Him to forgive you for being so selfish:

....

....

I am confident that you now have a better understanding of the importance of avoiding tithing with an attitude of expectancy. As you tithe, examine your motive and ensure that love is the reason for tithing.

Step 4

After giving your tithes, stop worrying about the sacrifice you made in giving and where the money is going to come from to pay your outstanding bills.

When you do that you kill the seed you have sown (your tithe) with worrying.

I will prove this to you using the farmer as an example:

If the farmer sows a corn seed and is overly concerned as to how the seed will germinate and decides to dig up the seed to observe this process he would have destroyed the future plant. That farmer would not know how many ears of corn he would have gotten from that seed.

Remind yourself, God loves a cheerful giver and do not destroy your future crops by a preoccupation with possible sources (or even the temptation to withhold your tithe) that could provide the shortfall that would be needed to fill the gap after paying your tithe.

Step 5

Live your life to the glory of God by obeying His commandments which include loving one another, avoiding covetousness and ....
....
(Complete the list of things you need to do in the space provided).

This step is a reminder that tithing is not an isolated event and so do not expect that once this is done your blessings will overflow.

Let us go back to the example using the farmer. The farmer sows his seed in the soil, it germinates and so he is looking forward to a bumper harvest but this might not materialize.

What are some of the reasons for the bumper harvest failing to materialize?

The farmer forgot to remove the weeds from his field. 'Weeds' are the sinful thoughts that we allow to grow that destroy our blessings from God. These 'weeds' might include thoughts of envy, lust, greed and selfishness. Whatever these are, God is not pleased and so He might withhold our blessings.

'Pests' usually leave their trail and marks on the plants. Let me point out that I am not a farmer so if I am not one hundred per cent accurate in my analysis, please give me credit for the principle highlighted in this example.

Pests, on the other hand, are seen in our lives through the bitterness, anger and ....
....
(Include other ways in which 'pests' can be seen in your life).

Haven't we all from time to time wondered after giving our tithes about the reasons we have not been as blessed as others.

Yes, indeed we are concerned as to the reasons that might have prevented our blessings.

As human beings we sometimes find it difficult to accept that our thoughts, attitudes and actions are preventing our blessings. Remember God's Word:

If I regard iniquity in my heart, the Lord will not hear me.

~ Psalm 66:18

The key word in that verse, 'regard', is sending a strong message to us from God. Regard means, thinking. Thinking iniquity according to this verse, blocks our prayers to God (The Lord will not hear me). If thinking has such a profound negative impact, can you imagine what happens when you start acting in ways displeasing to God?

Let us all do our self analysis so our 'spiritual farm' will abound with both spiritual and temporal fruits to the glory of God.

However there are times when persons do not experience financial blessings and yet they are obedient to God. Some persons make bad financial investments, procrastinate and refuse to get expert guidance..
....

(Include other reasons in the space provided).

In addition, there are times of spiritual testing as it was with Job when things do not seem to work out financially. So, please do not conclude that when blessings are not abounding then sin is. Communicate with God and analyze your life to see if you have done anything wrong and if not continue to obey God and wait on Him patiently.

Step 6

Repeat from steps 1 to 5 as you tithe in subsequent weeks, months...
....

(Include how you earn your income in the space provided).

The discipline in tithing is somewhat difficult to maintain when we face challenges which include arrears in our mortgages, motor vehicle payments, others............................
....

(Include your challenges in the space provided).

During these challenging periods you are afraid of letting go of your scarce resources. You believe that God might not provide for you and fear being financially embarrassed.

Continue to tithe on a regular basis as you were doing before you faced these challenges.

Please do not miss a single opportunity to tithe. Exercise your faith in God not your fear (re-read chapter 5 on Faith).

In time you will experience God's goodness in helping you to overcome your challenges.

Be thankful to God at all times and resist the temptation to use tithing as a bargaining tool as previously discussed.

OFFERRING

A frequently asked question is, what is the difference between tithe and offering?

- Tithing, as stated before, is giving a specific percentage, (one tenth) of your gross earnings before any deduction given as a command by God to be adhered to by us.
- Offering as the name suggests, is an offer to God of an amount determined and given willingly by an individual.

God substantiates the objective of an offering in the Old Testament:

Then the Lord spoke to Moses saying: "Speak to the children of Israel, that they bring Me an offering. From everyone who gives it willingly with his heart you shall take my offering."

~ Exodus 25: 1–2

When giving your offering, bear in mind at all times that God loves a cheerful giver. In other words, don't give because you believe you have to and murmur when you do it. Do it cheerfully not grudgingly. I know you have not forgotten but I will use this opportunity to reiterate; when you give to God your tithe comes first and this is separate from your offering which you determine.

GIVING GENERALLY

You have given your tithes and your offering and you might not see the need to give to anyone else.

Again I remind you of the verse highlighted above on cheerful giving as well as God's command for us to love one another. We should never forget that God is a God of community He loves us all and teaches us to demonstrate our love to each other. Giving is an example of demonstrating love.

God also highlights to us that when we give, it is not a futile effort, our gifts will come back to us in one way or another. At times we might not even be aware that this is happening:

Cast your bread upon the waters, for you will find it after many days.

Ecclesiastes 11:1

According to Ecclesiastes, our giving is never lost. God sees and knows everything we do and our motives should be 'pure'. What do I mean by this? You have heard it before, give because you love and not out of a desire to receive.

I know you are all excited to give now!

So, enjoy giving and include it always on your list of things that you need to do to demonstrate your obedience to God.

Give and watch your gifts bring joy to someone or your tithe help to meet the shortfall in the church's budget.

When you feel selfish and find it difficult to give, please remember the Word of God:

"It is more blessed to give than to receive."

~ Acts 20:35

THE WORD

In summary, giving is an act of love which is selfless as you share. Receiving is an act about self which can lead to selfishness as you hoard (give me, me, me!)

God demonstrates love to us as an action word:

For God so loved the world that He gave His only begotten son that whoever believes in Him should not perish but have everlasting life.

~ John 3:16

When you give, you demonstrate love.

When you receive from God and keep your gifts, you demonstrate selfishness.

Give and be blessed.

– 18 –

Idolatry

What do you think of when you hear the word idolatry?

As a child I imagined someone bowing down before an inanimate object, whether of wood, stone or some other material.

I suppose that was natural as I related it to the bible story where Aaron took all the golden earrings from the Israelites while Moses was on the mountain with God and melted them to make a golden calf. I can recall how the Israelites worshipped the golden calf as if it were responsible for taking them out of Egypt and bringing them into the wilderness:

> *So all the people broke off the golden earrings which were in their ears, and brought them to Aaron. And he received the gold from their hand, and he fashioned it with an engraving tool, and made a molded calf. Then they said, "This is your god, O Israel, that brought you out of the land of Egypt!"*
>
> *~ Exodus 32: 3–4*

An idol is worshipped or adored. However, we need to remember that adoration should be reserved only for God, our

THE WORD

Creator and Creator of the universe. God reminds us of this in His Word:

> *You shall have no other gods before Me. You shall not make for yourself a carved image – any likeness of anything that is in heaven above, or that is in the earth beneath, or that is in the water under the earth; you shall not bow down to them nor serve them. For I, the Lord your God, am a jealous God, visiting the iniquity of the fathers upon the children to the third and fourth generations of those who hate Me.*
>
> *~ Exodus 20:3–5*

God knows what we are capable of doing and so He provides specific instructions to serve as a reminder for us not to make and worship carved images. Are carved images the only thing that is worshipped by us as human beings?

Let us consider the dictionary's definition of an idol to guide us in answering the aforementioned question.

According to *The Little Oxford Dictionary and Thesaurus*, an idol is an image worshipped as a god or an idolized person or thing. Based on the dictionary's definition, idolatry would not only include worshipping carved images but human beings as well as objects or things.

What a surprise! For those of us who are not literally bowing down and worshipping a carved image and therefore think we are not guilty of idol worshipping, I am about to prove you wrong if there are other things that consume your life. When you worship someone or something, you always focus your attention on that person or thing. In other words, you spend a significant amount of your time thinking about or being with your idol.

Let us go back to the dictionary's definition and use some

IDOLATRY

examples to cement our understanding of how human beings and objects are treated as idols. Human beings would include our partners (husband, wife, girlfriend, boyfriend), our children, prominent persons in the society and others ....
....
(Include other persons you deem idols).

Objects or things would include our lovely homes, cars, jobs, jewellery (diamond, pearls, gold other................................... (add your choice), bank account and..
....
(Include other things that consume your time and energy).

- Have you ever found yourself almost literally worshipping the ground your partner walks on?

You would do anything just to be with this person. You have stopped going to church because the person is not a Christian and wants you to go to the beach on Sunday. Yes! That is idol worshipping. You have chosen this person, your idol, over worshipping God. You have actually given that individual the first place in your life that should have been reserved for God. I know you might want to justify your actions by stating that when you go to the beach with that person you use it as an opportunity to witness to him or her about Christ. You know that would not be the truth so read your bible and pray to God to help you to be a true witness for Him by inviting this person to church with you. If he or she refuses your invitation let the individual understand that God is the one you worship and adore. What about your sons or daughters that you continuously boast about? You are so consumed by your children that you pamper and refuse to discipline. To justify your action you claim that you do not want to hurt them or damage their self esteem. I have a subtle reminder for you; your children are gifts from God and are not meant to be idols. Let's recall God's Word about your responsibility:

> *Train up a child in the way he should go, and when he is old he will not depart from it*
>
> *~Proverbs 22:6*

Your response with explanation to the questions below will help to determine if you are guilty of idolatry with any prominent person in the society. Do you avoid going to prayer meetings during the week because you find it difficult to refuse an invitation to a social event with a prominent person in your society?

Your response..

Do you spend excessively (beyond your current and future budget) just to socialize with such a person?

Your response..

Our actions towards prominent persons in the society can be an indication of where our loyalty lies. Sometimes we are so focused on climbing the social ladder that we forget the spiritual consequences.

Let us bear in mind Jesus' reminder:

> *For where your treasure is, there your heart will be also.*
>
> *~ Matthew 6:21*

Examine the following examples of idolatry:

- You have been praying to God to bless you with an expensive motor vehicle and He has blessed you with a .... (Include the car of your choice). Before you owned the car you would visit church frequently including weekly prayer meetings, sing on the choir and perform in other church activities. However, since you have become the owner of this expensive car, you cannot find the time to go to church. You cannot even find the time to pray to God anymore as you are just preoccupied and consumed with this car . . . Your idol! Oh yes, you might say it is not so and try to justify visiting friends on the weekend instead of going to church. Answer the question: Is this car an idol? You know your answer and you know what God says about idolatry.

- You realize that you have millions of dollars in your bank account. You have always dreamed of becoming a millionaire and now this is a reality. You currently spend a lot of time thinking of possible investments you could make to increase your cash position. As a result, your prayers are often interrupted as you stop to make telephone calls or discuss ideas that pop into your head to make you wealthier.

Is that idolatry?

I would think so . . .

Do you?

The examples give us an idea of the mistakes we make when we devote an excessive amount of our time, effort and money to things that are created instead of our creator.

In our lives we are all guilty of some acts that could be deemed as idolatry in which we have rationalized our actions in order to justify our desires.

Let us make the change today to adhere to God's Word and give Him the glory as our Creator and avoid idolatry.

– 19 –

Religion

Let us go on a journey to the Garden of Eden and learn more about Adam and Eve . . . Adam and Eve exercised their freedom of choice and disobeyed God's command by eating the fruit and were chased out of the garden:

> *Therefore the Lord God sent him out of the garden of Eden to till the ground from which he was taken.*
>
> *~ Genesis 3:23*

God knew that the freedom of choice meant that Adam and Eve could return to the garden despite being chased out. God could have prevented them from returning to the garden by removing their free will. Instead of removing their free will God ensured that the tree was guarded to prevent them from picking the fruit:

> *So, He drove out the man; and He placed cherubim at the east of the garden of Eden, and a flaming sword which turned every way, to guard the way to the tree of life.*
>
> *~ Genesis 3:24*

We have just come to the end of our short journey. What

have you learnt and how does it relate to this chapter? Include your response in the space provided:

....

....

Yes, we all have the right to exercise our freedom of choice and this also includes our religion. God's action substantiates the point that you should allow persons to exercise their freedom of choice and not force them to accept your religion which includes the day of worship and denomination.

In exercising our freedom of choice, if we accept the plan of salvation provided by Jesus Christ, Our Lord and Saviour we thereby declare ourselves Christians. On the other hand, there are persons who believe in other religions.

What is interesting is that our free will means, it is our choice and not God's choice for us that determines our eternal status.

God does not force us to become Christians. God yearns for us to understand that He loves us and only wants the best for us and so He constantly reminds us in His Word that our actions will determine our eternal status.

In helping us to make the right choice, God guides us through the Bible, His ministers, evangelists, ...

....

(Include other ways in which you learn about God). Regardless of the ways in which we learn about God all sources attest to the existence and power of God. Do you agree?

What we need to do is to let our light shine following the example that Jesus has set for us by being obedient to God, avoiding the sins that God highlights in His Word and loving our neighbours, regardless of religion, race, class and the list is endless . . .

- What message is God's approach sending to us?

When our life becomes a shining example, others will attest to the fact that our God is the true and living God. The principle in Elijah's approach on Mount Carmel in determining the True and Living God and by extension his religion provides an example that we can emulate. I will provide a brief summary of what transpired before we examine the Bible passages:

Elijah, the only prophet of God at the time, found himself outnumbered by the false prophets of baal as, there were four hundred and fifty of them. Can you imagine the outcome if a vote was taken based on the census as to who was the True and Living God? Elijah's God would have lost. However, it is not the number of persons who declare their support that determines the winner. Instead, it is the power demonstrated by the True and Living God. If you agree, say, "Amen." Continuing . . . .

Elijah suggested to the children of Israel and baal's false prophets that two sacrifices should be placed on the altar, one for baal and one for the Lord. He further stated that baal's prophets should make a request to their gods to consume their sacrifice and He would pray to the Lord God to do likewise with his sacrifice.

Elijah and baal's prophets agreed that the God who consumed the sacrifice would be declared the True and Living God.

We will now examine the relevant scripture passages:

Then Elijah said to the people, "I alone am left, a prophet of the Lord; but Baal's prophets are four hundred and fifty men. "Therefore, let them give us two bulls; and let them choose one bull for themselves, cut one in pieces and lay it on the wood, but put no fire under it; and I will prepare

> *the other bull, and lay it on the wood but put no fire under it. "Then you call on the name of your gods and I will call on the name of the Lord; and the God who answers by fire, He is God." So all the people answered and said, "It is well spoken."*
>
> ~ *1 Kings 18: 22–23*

Elijah waited until the prophets of baal called on their gods to send fire to consume the sacrifice. They called on their gods from morning to the evening sacrifice without any fire descending to consume the sacrifice.

Elijah mocked them by encouraging them to continue to call on their gods. Elijah even suggested reasons that could contribute to the fact that their gods were not able to hear them:

> *And so it was at noon, that Elijah mocked them and said, "Cry aloud, for he is a god, either he is meditating or he is busy, or he is on a journey, or perhaps he is sleepy and must be awakened."*
>
> ~ *1 Kings 18:27*

I want you to note, Elijah referred to their god with a common 'g'. *The Little Oxford and Dictionary Thesaurus* defines god (with the common 'g') as, 'super human being worshipped as having power over nature and human affairs'.

Our God with a capital 'G' is defined by the dictionary as, 'creator and ruler of the universe'. Can you now make the connection with what Elijah was saying to the prophets of baal?

I believe Elijah was highlighting to the prophets of baal in a subtle way the fact, their god is a created being and that there is only one God, The Creator. This means that their god could only be human like themselves doing the things they do including meditating, travelling, or sleeping and would need to be awakened. In other words their 'common' god, (baal) is no match for His 'Capital' God.

I can imagine how embarrassed these prophets were as they leapt upon the altar, cried aloud and cut themselves with knives and lancets until the blood gushed upon them.

Elijah was about to prove to the prophets of baal who is the True and Living God. However, before doing, so Elijah demonstrated an important act. He repaired the altar of the Lord that was broken down. Translated in our context today, this means before you call on God ensure that you confess sins that have separated you from Him, and reconcile with your brothers and sisters where necessary. Remember God's Word declares:

If I regard iniquity in my heart, the Lord will not hear.

~ Psalm 66:18

What was Elijah's approach?

Elijah made a trench around the altar, requested four barrels of water to saturate the sacrifice and the wood and repeated this three times. Finally he filled the trench with water.

The real test of the True and Living God is that when the circumstances look impossible to the human eyes, God's power then shines through impossibilities to leave us in awe at who He is, the Great I Am.

Before I expound on Elijah's action on Mount Carmel I want to remind you that there is no need to fight to prove which day of worship or denomination is the true one. Elijah demonstrated the correct approach by relying on the power of God to prove the point:

RELIGION

And it came to pass, at the time of the offering of the evening sacrifice, that Elijah the prophet came near and said, "Lord God of Abraham, Isaac and Israel let it be known this day that you are God in Israel and I am Your servant and that I have done all these things at Your word. Hear me O Lord, hear me, that this people may know that You are the Lord God and that You have turned their hearts back to You again."

~ 1 Kings 18: 36-37

Let me interrupt the flow of the verses to make an important point. Elijah did not fight with the prophets of baal and engage in a war with words to prove his point.

What did he do? He prayed to God to demonstrate His power so that the people would know that He is the True and Living God.

What happened next? Fireworks!

Then the fire of the Lord fell and consumed the burnt sacrifice and the wood and the stones and the dust, and it licked up the water that was in the trench.

~ 1 Kings 18:38

Remember what I said earlier, stop the fighting over religion. Repair the altar of the Lord by living your life according to His Holy standard and then ask Him to manifest Himself to those whom you want to know that your God is the True and Living God. Look what happened next with Elijah:

Now when all the people saw it, they fell on their faces, and they said "The Lord, He is God! The Lord, He is God!"

~ 1 Kings 18:39

Please note, Elijah did not have to force anyone to acknowledge God as the True and Living God as God's display of power was truly awesome. Can you promise me that after today you will stop fighting to prove which religion is the right one?

Yes? I hope you really mean that. Remember Jesus' words to His disciples which apply to us as well:

> *Go ye therefore and teach all nations, baptizing them in the name of the Father and of the Son and of the Holy Ghost. Teaching them to observe all things whatsoever I have commanded you: and I am with you always, even to the end of the age. Amen*
>
> *~ Matthew 28: 19-20 (KJV)*

Note, Jesus said, "we are to teach", not fight, not impose, not threaten, not abuse. What is teaching? According to the Little Oxford Dictionary and Thesaurus, to teach means, impart information or skill to a person or about a subject. Expressed simply, share the good news. Your role then is to share the good news genuinely and if that person rejects Christ that individual has exercised his or her freedom of choice with the inherent consequence (missing out on eternal life and receiving eternal damnation instead). An important reminder, you have no right to impose, your role is to inform. When you have shared the good news, then like Elijah, pray for them.

Many persons become defensive and more resistant to the Word of God when you pray for them openly. In such instances, practise praying for them the way Jesus taught us to pray in secret:

> *"But you, when you pray, go into your room and when you have shut your door, pray to your Father who is in the secret place, and your Father who sees in secret will reward you openly"*
>
> *~ Matthew 6:6*

Reiterating, God our Creator has never forced us to do that which our free will resists. He guides us like He did Adam and Eve, showing them what they should do (fruits of the trees they could eat), what they needed to avoid (the fruits of the tree in the midst of the garden) and the harm that would come to them if they disobeyed (death).

Adam and Eve exercised their free will and disobeyed. We have all suffered as a result of their decision. However, Jesus the Living Lamb of God redeemed us and He is worthy of our praise. How does the redemption plan help you as you share the good news of Christ?

For persons that you witness to who exercise their free will and refuse to accept Christianity as their religion they will still be able to benefit from Christ's redemption plan if later they are willing to embrace Christianity.

What an awesome God; He never rejects us despite our rejection of Him. Instead, He waits with open arms to receive us when our choice embraces His gift of redemption.

I leave you to ponder your actions and consider whether these have caused harm or have been beneficial to those you want to share your religion with.

Do your soul search using the following passage:

Let your light so shine before men, that they may see your good works and glorify your Father in heaven.

~Matthew 5:16

- Is your light shining or have your actions put it out?
- Can you honestly state that your works are good?

Please let God decide who are worthy of eternal life. Jesus

explains this to us in the parable of the sower where He states that both the wheat and the tares should grow together until the day of harvest:

> *Let both grow together until the harvest, and at the time of harvest I will say to the reapers, "First gather together the tares and bind them in bundles to burn them, but gather the wheat into my barn*
>
> *~ Matthew 13: 30*

It is not our role to determine which religion is right or wrong so let us stop being judgmental and heed the warning of Jesus who will be our judge:

> *Judge not, that ye be not judged. For with what judgment you judge you will be judged; and with the measure you use it will be measured back to you.*
>
> *~ Matthew 7:1-2*

Are your guilty of judging another with regards to religion? I will make my confession, I know I am guilty. What we all need to do, however, is to ask God to help us to stop being judges and see ourselves as sinners. We need to humble ourselves before God so we can take the necessary corrective actions by confessing our sins, adhering to God's command including loving our neighbours and thereby allowing others to see the quality of our 'fruit'.

God reminds us that we should not only declare His name but we should also do His will:

> *Not everyone who says to me, Lord, Lord, shall enter the Kingdom of heaven, but he who does the will of My Father in heaven.*
>
> *~ Matthew 7:21*

Ouch! Ouch! The passage states, 'not everyone that says 'Lord shall enter.' Be careful, ensure that you are sincere in the sight of God. Always ask yourself these two questions:

- What is my motive?
- Is my motive pleasing to God?

Do not wait until Jesus takes out His books on the events of your life and reminds you of the number of times you were 'holy' in your words trying to prove which religion is correct but sinful in your actions.

Make the change now so that when Jesus goes through His books to determine your fate, your actions will lead to eternal life and not eternal damnation.

Additionally engage in acts of kindness so you will be welcomed by Jesus into His kingdom:

Then the King will say to those on His right hand, 'Come, you blessed of My Father, inherit the kingdom prepared for you from the foundation of the world: for I was hungry and you gave Me drink; I was a stranger and you took Me in; I was naked and you clothed Me; I was sick and you visited Me; I was in prison and you came to Me.

~ Matthew 25: 34–36

Please do not go looking for Jesus to do acts of kindness to. Jesus expects us to love one another and demonstrate our love for Him through these acts to each other regardless of race, religion, class or colour:

And the King will answer and say to them, 'Assuredly, I say to you, inasmuch as you did it to one of the least of these My brethren, you did it to me.'

~ Matthew 25:40

THE WORD

Let us all do the will of God including Jesus' command to teach the gospel and cease from our personal assignment of trying to prove which religion is right or wrong.

Let your light shine brightly reflecting the sincerity of your faith in Christ and your respect for your fellow human beings freedom of choice.

– 20 –

Timely Reminders

Some things you need to be reminded of:

1. God is aware of everything that happens to you in life.

   Experiences in life provide opportunities for growth if we do not allow ourselves to be immobilized or embittered by these.

2. Do not allow material things to be your master as you automatically become the slave.

   The more you have of material things is the more you desire resulting in sleepless nights, broken family relationships and eventually a toll on your physical health. In the meantime, you would have been too busy focusing on your material goals so you would have ignored your spiritual health. If you continue at this pace eventually you will die and lose out both physically and spiritually.

3. Do not destroy your life if someone does not love you.

   God expects us to love one another. Remember, however, you cannot force others to love you. Focus your attention on God, your creator and on Jesus, your Saviour who loves you. Jesus will heal your hurt.

Strengthen your relationship with God through prayer, fasting and the reading of the Word.

Use your gifts and talents to help others. Shower your love on someone who needs it and not on someone you believe you need. When you are the victim of unrequited love, the tendency is to feel sorry for yourself and try to impress or grovel hoping that the other person returns your love. This is futile as love is a gift given freely as God demonstrated. If you have to coerce, impress or be desperate, it is not worth it:

For God so loved the world that he gave His only begotten Son.

~ John 3:16

4. Money does not make you happy. Money enables you to acquire the things you need or desire. Be careful how you idolize money as it prevents you from worshipping God as eventually you will become too busy either making or spending money:

   For the love of money is a root of all kinds of evil which some have strayed from the faith in their greediness and pierced themselves through with many sorrows.

   ~ 1 Timothy 6:10

5. Idols cannot have relationships. If you worship other human beings they certainly will not be able to relate to you as you have dehumanized them. Humans are created beings, only God is worthy of and appreciates our acts of worship. If you

doubt this fact just read the comments of some persons who have attempted to idolize persons in their relationship: 'After all I did for him or her, worshipping the ground he or she walks on and then to be rejected in this manner. That's natural . . . we do not and will never learn to handle being idolized as we are mere mortals and so our natural tendency is to reject persons who idolize us by humiliating, ignoring, abusing or ....
....

(include other ways you have experienced rejection in the space provided). Always remember we are created and so all adoration should only be to our Creator, God.

6. We believe God does not care when our selfish actions result in human suffering. God has given us the freedom to choose. If our fellow human beings choose evil over good then we all suffer the consequences of their choice. So when there are major sufferings that result from the way we treat each other including senseless killings, rape, starvation, we claim that God does not care. The truth is, we are the ones who do not care. So let us start taking responsibility for our actions and change our ways and love one another.

7. Rape, abuse, gun violence and suicide are destructive ways in which we vent our problems/issues. God has provided words for us to express ourselves in sharing our feelings and allowing us to empathize with each other.

There are also many persons whom God has blessed with the ability to help us cope with our pain so our issues/problems do not have to be translated into rape, abuse, gun violence or suicide.

THE WORD

Start talking now!! Regardless of the nature of the problem, there is no need for embarrassment.

Many other persons share similar issues and God reminds us about this in His Word:

> *No temptation has overtaken you except such as is common to man; but God is faithful, who will not allow you to be tempted beyond what you are able, but with the temptation will also make the way of escape, that you may be able to bear it.*
>
> *~ 1 Corinthians 10:13*

You will become a victor when you overcome your issues/problems and share your testimony with others who are facing similar trials to the ones you experienced.

Do not waste your life; God has a plan for you on this earth and you have a role to help someone. Start now!!

Timely reminders are necessary to help us in our areas of weaknesses. As we reiterate the things that we should or shouldn't do we reinforce in our minds the corrective actions that we need to take.

– 21 –

Conclusion

On introspection we should all be able to agree on at least one thing, that is, all of us have erred in one way or another.

As human beings we are all guilty sometimes of being angry, proud, discontented, unforgiving, ungrateful and the list is endless . . .

We can now reflect on the mistakes we have made and ask God's forgiveness and guidance in helping us to live according to His guiding principles.

Having read Part I, I hope that you will all be better able to understand the impact of your actions on your interpersonal relationships. You should be willing to forgive and in like manner seek forgiveness where this is necessary.

Chapter 12, "Nature's Lesson on Patience, Humility and Pride" shown through the moth and the lizard is a profound reminder of the importance of self-acceptance which should translate into humility and patience as demonstrated by the lizard. Pride, as demonstrated by the moth, Powers us to our destruction and sometimes to our demise.

Abiding by God's guiding principles as demonstrated in part

THE WORD

1 will enable us to improve our relationship with God and our fellow human beings.

With our religion, our aim should be to share the good news not to attempt to prove who is right or wrong.

God bless you in your efforts to apply His guiding principles in your life.

– PART II –
GOD'S PLAN OF SALVATION

(From Creation to Eternity)

Where did I come from?

And the Lord God formed man of the dust of the ground, and breathed into His nostrils the breath of life; and man became a A living soul.

Genesis 2:7 (NKJV)

Who created me?

For by Him all things were created that are in heaven and that are on earth, visible and invisible, whether thrones or dominions or principalities or powers. All things were create through Him and for Him.

Colossians 1:16 (NKJV)

Why do I have to die?

Nevertheless death reigned from Adam to Moses, even over those who had not sinned according to the likeness of the transgression of Adam, who is a type of Him who was to come.

Romans 5:14 (NKJV)

Does it all end when I die?

And it is appointed for men to die once, but after this the Judgment.

Hebrews 9:27 (NKJV)

What will judgment be like?

And I saw the dead, small and great, standing before God and books were opened. And another book was opened which is the Book of Life. And the dead were judged according to their works, by the things which were written in the books. And anyone not found written in the Book of Life was cast into the lake of fire.

Revelation 20: 12, 15 (NKJV)

How can I enjoy eternal life and avoid the lake of fire?

For God so loved the world that He gave His only begotten Son, that whoever believes in Him should not perish but have everlasting life.

John 3:16 (NKJV)

Do You Believe?

Lord, I believe; help my unbelief!

Mark 9: 24 (NKJV)

Part II is dedicated to the memory of
my mother, Hyacinth May Allen and my father, Frederick Nathaniel
Allen; they taught me the importance of having faith in God.
Their constant reminder that God is always there to help me
through life's challenges has been a source of inspiration:

"Lo, I am with you always, even unto the end of the world."

~ Matthew 28: 20

– 22 –

Introduction

As you read Part II of this book which is an exposition of the first thirteen verses of St. John chapter 1 you will see that I have taken the time to provide you with other scripture passages that will aid in a better understanding of God's plan of salvation. Most of the scripture passages quoted are from the King James version of the Bible. Other scripture passages used from the New King James version are included as NKJV.

Part II will help you to understand the impact of sin in your lives, teach you how to change from a sinful lifestyle and remain faithful to God so that you will be able to live a victorious life in this world and ultimately enjoy eternal life.

It is important for my readers to know that Jesus is also referred to as "The Living Word". Why the Living Word? Remember we cannot see God and so God as a Spirit guides us through His Word. Jesus, on the other hand, came on earth as a human being living amongst us. Today, He guides us using the Word of God and whilst on earth communicated in the context of the times in which He lived and the people He lived amongst. Jesus spoke in parables using sheep and the fig tree

INTRODUCTION

as examples of some of the things that those persons could relate to.

Jesus, as a physical being, could be touched; He expressed emotion when He cried at the death of Lazarus. Jesus, indeed, is the Living Word.

A popular question asked with regards to Jesus is, "Did He exist with God, The Father at creation?"

This question is answered in chapter 32, entitled, "The Mystery of the Father and The Son" which will help you to understand that Jesus has always co-existed with His Father.

Since creation, communication has been vital in the relationship which humans have with God. He communicates with us in many ways which include the Bible, His angels, His prophets and Jesus, The Living Word, His Son.

Today, God continues to speak to us through the Holy Bible. Obedience to the Word of God is vital for our spiritual growth. We should always be receptive to God's Word and thereby ensure that our lives are pleasing to Him.

I know many persons are very unhappy with their lives but would rather live in denial by pretending to be happy whilst doing the wrong things. Some persons are using alcohol, drugs and parties to run away from the emptiness they feel inside. Running is tiring and there is no medal to be received for your efforts.

You are probably scared to tell Jesus how you feel because you are afraid your friends will laugh at you when they find out about your spiritual conversion.

I assure you, the only regrets you will have if you turn to Jesus today is that you did not do so earlier.

THE WORD

Please take time to read Part II slowly, examining the choices available and the respective consequences for each choice.

Promise me that you will read every page and you will not cheat. If you cheat, who knows? The page you omit might be the page that would have resulted in transforming your life.

God bless you all!

– 23 –

Knowing God

"In the beginning was the Word, and the Word was with God, and the Word was God."

~John 1:1 (NKJV)

Jesus is described as the Living Word as He came on earth and dwelt as a human being like us and used words to communicate with us. In Genesis chapter one, God used words to create the heaven and the earth. Words then are means of communication used by God, The Father, and Jesus the Son, The Living Word.

Jesus has always coexisted with God, The Father, from the very beginning.

Beginning is defined by *The Little Oxford Dictionary and Thesaurus* as source or origin. God is therefore the source of creation. He is the creator, everything begins and ends with Him. What is important is not when God created but that He created.

God is a Spirit and so He cannot be seen with our naked eyes. God communicates with us and keeps His promises as He cannot lie. God and His words are therefore inseparable. When

God speaks, we know it is God as His promises are kept. He never fails.

Interestingly, as human beings, we make promises but we do not always keep these promises. People often pledge in their marriage that they will be together until they are separated by death. In many instances, however, they are separated by divorce.

You could not say, then, that such persons are inseparable from their words, as they are; they change. God, however, never changes so when He says, "I am with you always even to the end of the age" (St. Matthew 28: 20), God means every word so whether you are happy or sad, successful or unsuccessful God is with you and will continue to be with you all the time.

To establish a relationship with God we first have to know that God can be relied on, God can be trusted. It is therefore important to accept this fact and let it sink deep in our hearts that God is not like man. When we believe this we will be able to hold on by faith regardless of our circumstances. We must not doubt.

It will be difficult to have faith if we do not accept that God is the source of our lives. Importantly, God cannot be separated from His words. Always remember, God cannot lie.

Why am I saying this? Let us look at an example. Let's say you are going through a rough patch financially and you are unable to pay your rent or mortgage and this has been happening for a number of months. God's Word tells us to call upon Him and He will hear us. The same faithful God who spoke to Jeremiah while he was in prison is saying to us today the very words He spoke to Jeremiah, "Call to me, and I will answer you and show you great and mighty things which you do not know" (Jeremiah 33: 3).

You might ask the question, How are God's words going to help to pay my rent or mortgage?

Listen to His voice and you will find out.

Stop complaining! When you are talking you miss the gentle voice of Jesus. When you do, it's your fault. He spoke but you did not listen. God could be giving you ideas to generate additional income, or sending you to someone He has provided to assist you. God could even be giving you specific words to relay to your landlord or mortgage institution that would give you more time to work through your financial crisis. If you are busy doubting then you would have missed the opportunity to hear His words and to experience His faithfulness. Just remember when the storms of life rage, "He will never leave you nor forsake you" (Hebrew 13: 5).

When you are faced with trials and you pray and nothing seems to change remember do not conclude that God has let you down. What you are trying to do is to separate God from His Word and you cannot. What you have succeeded in doing is to separate yourself from His Word. Let us emphasize the point here, God is faithful and He will come true if you are faithful and believe.

We have the assurance regardless of what we face in our lives that God and His Son, Jesus, have always existed and their words are always life transforming.

– 24 –

The Unchanging God

"He was in the beginning with God"

~ John 1:2 (NKJV)

Jesus confirmed that His relationship with God existed before the foundation of the world when He said: "Father, I will that they also whom thou hast given me be with me where I am; that they may behold my glory, which thou hast given me: for thou lovedst me before the foundation of the world" (John 17: 24).

Further evidence is provided that serves as confirmation that Jesus was present at creation with God as God used the plural tense: "Then God said, "Let Us make man in Our image, according to Our likeness . . ."" (Genesis 1: 26).

In the Bible, we first meet God in Genesis Chapter 1 where we learnt about God's role in creation. God's words were instrumental at the very foundation of the world. Let us now look briefly at the creation story and the importance of God's words in this at the very beginning.

It was God's spoken words that brought everything into being at creation. I know, it is somewhat of a mystery to accept that everything started with God and that He has always been around. This is where faith comes in as we have to accept that our God is the foundation of everything. Therefore, the beginning and God are inseparable.

The Word of God set in motion what we now have as heaven and earth.

Let us reiterate the point, God cannot be separated from His Word and this was so even at the beginning.

Friends, the heaven and the earth could not have evolved. God is definitely responsible for this beautiful creation. He alone could have given us the beauty, the precision and details of the universe and its contents including the animals that we now enjoy. Our God is definitely in control. God cares so much about the animals He created which do not have a soul so this should serve as confirmation to us that God loves us and is always working on our behalf. The birds are always very chirpy because God takes care of their food. He provides the trees with food and He also provides us as human beings to feed them. Let us remind ourselves of this important fact that God is working on our behalf not sometimes but all the times despite our feelings or our circumstances.

Let us now try to comprehend what God did at creation.

To imagine what the earth had looked like before God's spoken words just think about an all island power cut that you were not prepared for . . . . Suddenly everything is black. . . . Darkness has taken over . . . . You cannot see anything . . . . There is no shape . . . no form. Can you imagine what this earth was like before God's words? It was scary.

What an awesome God to be able to speak words to give us this beautiful universe we have today. That is God's power and

THE WORD

He is worthy to be praised.

We should never forget that electricity is one of God's gifts to us that He has revealed through the knowledge He has given to man.

In the same way God spoke the Words at creation to bring light out of darkness, He now speaks in our lives to bring light in the midst of our dark circumstances: loneliness, fear, unemployment, betrayal or any other issues that confront us. Let us remember in our darkest moment that God's Word brings action and light will follow. The light will bring changed circumstances turning sorrow into joy. We should bear in mind, however, that sometimes God does not change the circumstance completely but provides joy in the midst of our sorrow, peace in the midst of the storm. When God works like this He uses our circumstances to build our trust in Him. We also learn patience, tolerance and develop a sense of peace that only God gives which is unrelated to our circumstances. In times like these people will want to know reasons for your calmness even though you are unemployed, have been evicted by your landlord, rejected by your friends or any other trial that confronts you that you are able to cope with through God's grace.

Patience is often described as a virtue in a secular sense. This attribute is even more important spiritually. A lack of patience can be a demonstration of a lack of faith in God.

Please be patient! Do not be impulsive! God might not come through for you in a twenty four hour period, or even a whole year or more. Yes! that can happen. What we need to remember however, is that God is faithful and cannot be separated from His Word so, He will come through for you. Be patient you will not remain in darkness forever . . . the light will shine through. As you wait, demonstrate your faith in God by thanking Him for your deliverance that is on its way. I am confident, it will happen!!

We need to constantly remind ourselves as we study the Word of God that with God nothing changes over time so whether it is in Genesis, in the beginning at the creation or in John there is consistency with God and His Word. God's consistency is a very important point to note as in our spiritual life we often say that God only works for people in the Bible and He will not work for us today and help us with our challenges. Oh yes! He will! But are you, believing Him and His Word?

Look at the world today that God created, we still have the heavens, the earth, the seas and all the other things He created. Isn't that adequate evidence that God has not changed? God's words were there in the beginning with God and so shall it be at the end.

– 25 –

The Master Creator

"All Things were made through Him, and without Him nothing was made that was made"

~ John 1:3 (NKJV)

Everything on this earth has been made by God or made with His approval.

In our manufacturing industries everything that is used comes directly or indirectly from God's creation. The stone, lumber, mineral, agricultural products or gases, they were all made by God or processed through God's guidance.

You might look at your lovely home and say it was built by your contractor. Please tell me what did the contractor make? Everything he used would have already been provided by God. Oh yes, go right ahead, I know you are about to say that some of the things could not be used in the original form that God made it in and it had to be processed. Some examples are bauxite, diamond, gold and the timber from the trees. I agree totally that some amount of processing takes place but the knowledge to do this comes from God. If God does not reveal this knowledge to us, then our efforts would be futile.

THE MASTER CREATOR

Whatever we do, if God does not approve it through His revelation in the form of knowledge, then nothing happens. Can we now recognize our total dependence on God?

Yes, we should be ashamed of ourselves for taking credit for God's creation instead of giving Him the glory. It should be a humbling experience for us to acknowledge the mistakes we have made as we constantly reward human beings for their discoveries in science yet fail to acknowledge the one who is ultimately responsible for their success, Our Creator.

All of nature is obedient to God. God speaks with authority and when He does, whatever He says happens. Disobedience to God's spoken Word results in human suffering. So often, we read or observe that on many occasions we dump our river courses to make homes and then we end up with severe flooding. The river claims back its natural course. Why? We have tried to work against God's original plan and if it is not approved by God, disaster follows.

Reflecting on the number of times I have been fascinated by human beings' success using God's creation I now realize how I have failed to acknowledge God and His Word from the very beginning in the creation story. Take some time and do your own reflection . . . . Have you failed Him too or can you truly say that you have always been clear on the true meaning of St. John 1: 3?

God's creation should reinforce in our hearts that our eyes should be focused on God alone. Our hearts should be full of praise to Him for knowing our needs even before we have any idea of what these will be, providing for us and guiding us to achieve these things through His creation and the knowledge He reveals to us.

– 26 –

Life Giving

"In Him was life; and the life was the light of men"

~ John 1:4 (NKJV)

Let us search the scriptures to see the importance in our lives of the life of Jesus and the Light He brought to us as human beings and how Christ has saved us from death (spiritual) and darkness (sin).

To truly understand how Jesus became our light we have to look back at what man's life was like before Jesus sacrificed His life. We recall from the Book of Genesis that God used to fellowship with Adam in the Garden of Eden. All this changed after he and his wife disobeyed God and yielded to the devil's temptation. Life literally became very difficult for Adam and his wife thereafter as they were chased out of the garden. Adam was told that he now had to toil to make a living. His wife, Eve would 'bring forth children in sorrow.' In the Old Testament, we saw the effects of sin; Adam's son Cain killed his brother Abel and many other evils were committed by mankind in those days. Eventually, God destroyed the earth by a flood saving only Noah, his family and a pair of every living creature.

That's how vile mankind had become! God saw no other way to deal with us but to destroy us in the flood.

Man, through Adam's sin, was therefore in darkness. Darkness is sin and this means separation from God. God is a Spirit and through Him we have the opportunity to experience eternal life. Eternal life cannot be experienced in a sinful state.

In order for man to have light or the opportunity of eternal life, man had to receive God's redemption. A life was literally needed as a sacrifice to free us from the bondage of sins. Jesus' sacrifice of His life on the cross gave mankind a new beginning. We are once again able to fellowship with God. Jesus' life has therefore provided hope or light for mankind to have their sins forgiven and to enjoy eternal life once we are obedient to God's Word.

Let us use an analogy of being in literal darkness with no electricity and compare this with the difference the light makes when the electricity is restored. In the dark, we may remain in one position and wait for the power to be restored. We may try to feel our way around in the dark which is usually to our detriment as we might fall and hurt ourselves or bump into some piece of furniture which could also be harmful. When the light comes back it means that we can see clearly. We are now able to see the things or the pieces of furniture that we had hurt ourselves on in the dark. The pain we experienced from hurting ourselves in the dark could motivate us to rearrange objects in the room in such a manner that we would be less likely to hurt ourselves again if there was another power outage.

Once the light is back, we are able to continue our regular routines that need electricity such as washing, ironing, using the computer or watching the television. Electricity then provides light helping us to see and hence avoid pitfalls as well as enabling us to carry out our tasks more efficiently.

Jesus is the spiritual light in our lives that helps us to avoid the pitfall of sin. We can look back at how we hurt ourselves because of sin and we can move forward to make the changes with our confession. The quality of our lives is greatly improved as we now have the hope of eternal life. God's Word enlightens our darkness by providing guidelines as to how we should live. We are now victorious through the light of Jesus.

Indeed, Jesus' life through the Word of God became the light of men. The Word is there to move us into fellowship with God: "If we confess our sins He is faithful and just to forgive us our sins, and to cleanse us from all unrighteousness" (1 John 1: 9).

What a revelation! God's Word has brought hope and new life to mankind.

Friends, let me remind you; we can now rearrange our lives in such a manner that we avoid the darkness of hell which would hurt us eternally.

We are given the opportunity to look at our lives in sin or in darkness and determine the changes we need to make through the life of Jesus and His Word. Jesus is not forcing us to make the change but we are aware of the consequences if we do not change and that should help us to make the right decision. We are cognizant of the fact that if we do not change our sinful ways, darkness means eternal damnation or going to hell. God's Word provides guidelines as to how to live with our neighbours, to pray and to fellowship with others.

At all times we must remember that there can be no separation between God and His Word and that God is faithful.

LIFE GIVING

Indeed, God is our life and our light. This truth is endorsed in many places in the Bible and one such passage is, "This is the message which we have heard from Him. And declare to you, that God is light, and in Him is no darkness at all" (1 John 1: 5).

– 27 –

The Blinding Effects of Sin

"And the light shines in the darkness and the darkness did not comprehend it."

~ John 1:5 (NKJV)

Has anyone ever done something nice for you or given you a gift that you believed you did not deserve and it has left you so puzzled that you have rewrapped it and put it away?

Would you say such a behaviour would be like having, 'the light shining' on you, without your understanding why? In other words, the gift would not be beneficial to you because you did not accept the gift and use it to make a difference in your life. A little farfetched with the state of our economy, but let's say, someone gift wrapped a Mercedes Benz for you and you just could not understand how someone would think you are worthy of this. What would you do in that case? You might leave it in the garage and continue to take the bus (or would you?). If you continue to take the bus you would clearly not have understood the reason for the gift. Imagine! Someone cared about you enough to want you to stop taking the bus and to travel in comfort in an expensive car.

THE BLINDING EFFECTS OF SIN

The fact that you never understood the purpose of the gift means that you would continue with your usual lifestyle. So too, when we get the gift of salvation through the light of Jesus, if we understand, we confess our sins and change our life-style. If we do not, we remain in sin. It is okay, if you do not agree, challenge my statements but read on first . . . . The revelation of the power of Jesus in our sinful life is indeed a shining light, it brings hope. This hope translates into forgiveness of our sins and the opportunity to share eternal life with Jesus. If, however, we do not understand the redemptive power of Jesus, we will remain in darkness or hopelessness, in our sins.

Friends, we have a responsibility to ensure that we understand God's Word so we can move into the light. This understanding of God's Word comes when we ask questions of our fellow believers, read the Word of God, pray, fast and seek guidance from the Holy Spirit. If we hear the Word of God and are still in darkness, it means we are still living in sin. The Word of God has to have specific meaning in the life of an individual for the light of God to shine upon that person. In other words, we will have to recognize that our actions are wrong and that our sinful ways are preventing us from having a relationship with God. The word of God clearly states that God expects us to confess our sins and seek His forgiveness. God's Word also highlights the various sins and the consequences of these. We are therefore able to avoid sins' trap if we are obedient to God. Without a clear understanding of what God expects from us and the benefits we will receive from a relationship with God, we all remain in darkness.

So then, 'shining the light in the dark and the darkness comprehended not' means that sinners are not yet convinced that their lifestyle is wrong and needs changing. In the same way that shining a literal light in the dark is usually done for a specific purpose, so too the light of Jesus shines to provide, peace, salvation, grace and hope. When we share the good news about Jesus, we have a responsibility to ensure that the message is conveyed with specific meaning in the lives of those we witness to. If we fail to bring salvation on a personal note to these individuals all we would have done is to narrate the salvation story. We would then have failed in our role as witnesses. Our role is to help others to recognize their sinful state using the Word of God as our guide. Let me emphasize here that we cannot force people to accept Jesus in their lives as that is a personal decision. Our responsibility, however, is to ensure that we reveal everything we know about God's plan of salvation as we witness. Our explanations to others about salvation must be clear and reflect God's truth.

Always remember, however, that while God is ultimately responsible for the harvest, we have a responsibility to sow the seeds (the Word of God) and water them with prayer and fasting.

One profound fact that has come to light from this Bible study is that the sharing of the Gospel must be done in a meaningful way so that sinners can come to the throne of Grace with a full understanding that their salvation was bought with the blood of the Lamb. We are given a charge to reveal Jesus not only in words but in deed. When we do this, the world should see a difference in the way we conduct ourselves and our affairs as we too are a 'shining light' representing Jesus.

If any of my readers today has experienced God's light shining on them but refuse to accept God's plan of salvation, use this opportunity right now! Confess to Jesus your denial of Him and ask for His help in keeping your eyes focused on Him.

Without that Christian hope and without a correct understanding of what is expected of us we fall short of getting on the right track with God and will miss eternity.

All my readers should share that hope of eternal life because you have all received God's light.

I implore you friends, to ensure that, wherever God's light shines, that there is no darkness. It is important for you to start with your own lives as you cannot help anyone else if your salvation is not secure.

Salvation is personal. If you cannot relate it to your own lives as individuals, you will not be able to understand the great benefits to be derived through Christ's death on the cross.

Please spread the good news of the power of Jesus, and our hope in Him of salvation as you minister to others.

– 28 –

The Forerunner

"There was a man sent from God, whose name was John"

~John 1:6 (NKJV)

John is described as the forerunner of Jesus Christ. In other words, he came to give us the good news concerning the coming of Jesus Christ. In Luke chapter 1, we learn that John was the son of Elizabeth and Zacharias, the priest who were both very old. God blessed these two righteous people in their old age with a son although Elizabeth was barren. Six months later Mary, Elizabeth's cousin, received the good news that she would be the mother of Jesus.

To be the forerunner of Jesus, John had to be upright in order to tell people about the coming of Jesus. It is therefore understandable that John's character had to be impeccable. Can you imagine someone who had a bad character introducing the Saviour? I doubt that anyone would want to listen to him.

What an awesome experience it must have been for John's parents to be told that their son would be filled with the Holy Ghost even from his mother's womb. According to the angel, "For he will be great in the sight of the Lord, and shall drink neither wine nor strong drink. He will also be filled with the Holy Spirit, even from his mother's womb" (Luke 1: 15). This meant John would be filled with God's Spirit from his mother's womb, would be guided by God's Spirit and be ready to manifest God's truth at the appropriate time.

Friends, we should live our lives in such a manner that God will be able to use us as His witnesses to help persons who are lost in sin in our community and in the wider society. There are two things that stand out if we are to be truly used by God. Firstly, we need to live righteous lives. Secondly, we need to realize that our lifestyle also affects the lives of our offspring. John's parents were righteous people who strived to please God. God in return blessed them with a son whom He used in a mighty way. Do you believe God would have used the son of Elizabeth and Zacharias if they had led ungodly lives? Of course not! People form an association between an individual and those they are related to. That is a very significant lesson for us. Oh yes! You still keep a bottle of liquor stashed away and drink when no one is watching. Please do not forget that God watches us all the time and He does not even have to see us; He knows what we will do long before we do it. For those of you who are addicted to alcohol, remember God's words to John's parents through His angel. John should drink neither wine nor strong drink. What about lying, stealing, drug addiction, abusing and so many other sins we could name? These are no exception as God is watching us and we cannot represent Him if our lives remain unchanged. We tarnish the name of our God by our actions so be careful how you witness.

Did I hear someone say that they have always wanted their son or daughter to be a minister or a missionary? Do you think

THE WORD

God is pleased with you as a parent and a role model while you are committing sins in the closet at home in the presence of your children? God cannot be pleased. There is hope, however, as long as you clean up your act and your sins are in the history book. Oh yes!! God will use you. Your life will demonstrate to others that they are not alone with their drug addiction, gambling or other vice. You will be the example of what God can do through His transforming power. Your sins would be in the past and you would now be a witness of a changed life through God's grace. You, like John, in your own way can be regarded as, 'a man sent from God.'

What a privilege indeed to be a genuine witness of God. Let us all strive for that position.

– 29 –

The Chosen Witness

"This man came for a witness, to bear witness of the Light, that all through him might believe"

~ John 1:7 (NKJV)

John's role was to inform us of the coming Messiah and of His awesome power. Throughout our study there has been continuous reference to the Word of God and the fact that God cannot be separated from His Word. This means that God cannot lie and whatever He promises, He will do. Join me now in a quick review of Chapter 28. Remember the angel told Elizabeth that the baby would be filled with the Holy Ghost even from the womb (Luke 1: 15). Let us look at the power of God's spoken words. In Luke, chapter 1: 41 when Mary visited her cousin Elizabeth and spoke, the baby leapt in Elizabeth's womb and she was filled with the Holy Ghost, so too was baby John as stated by the angel.

This example demonstrated to us God's power through His words. Mary was the mother of Jesus and her voice was a channel through which God's words were communicated. Even in the womb John had experienced the power of God and was, therefore, as God ordained it, a justified witness to tell us about Jesus.

Ladies! There is another point that needs to be highlighted here. What affects you during pregnancy can also affect your unborn child or children. You have to be careful about who or what you are exposed to in both words and deeds. Mary was righteous and her voice was used by God in a significant way to affect baby John who leapt in his mother's womb.

Mother's reflect . . . on your association during pregnancy and the impact some of the words heard could have on your child or children. Fathers! I am sure you thought that I did not have any words for you. You are wrong! You too need to be careful of your words and actions towards the females in pregnancy and at all other times. Let me repeat; be careful how you treat the ladies at all times.

I am sure you will all agree with me that a witness is one who has seen or heard something that they can attest to. So far John fits this description since he leapt when he heard the voice of Mary, God's instrument for the birth of His only son.

Let's digress a little and look at our legal system. When a witness is brought in court to give evidence this person usually has information that will make a significant difference to the outcome of the case. In many instances a person is either condemned or freed based on the evidence given by the witness.

John, as a witness, is not here to provide any information to condemn us. He is here to tell us about Jesus, the only one who can free us from sins' darkness and bring us into light. Jesus is the Light of our salvation and eternal life. John as a witness has made us realize how important it is for us as Christ's witnesses to have impeccable characters. If John's character had been tainted, he could not have convinced anyone to believe him.

Since John is our first exposure to Jesus, we have to believe in him enough to believe that what he said was true. If John's words were doubted, then naturally it would be more difficult for some persons to believe Jesus.

As you witness for Christ, remember the world has a fair number of doubting Thomas.

The importance of the authenticity of the evidence provided by the witness, John, has been highlighted in this chapter. As Christians, the Word of God should be our guide and our lifestyle should demonstrate a Christ-like character.

– 30 –

Accepting Your Role

"He was not that Light, but was sent to bear witness of that Light"

~ John 1:8 (NKJV)

This verse is used to emphasize John's role. He was sent to bear witness of that Light. He was not that Light.

Human beings enjoy modeling or acting. We tend to enjoy being in a position of prominence. Often times the acting role becomes so real that we forget our true status. This happens in a secular sense as well as a spiritual sense. Without realizing it, we become less effective in our assignment as our emphasis is now on keeping up the charade. Let us use an example to illustrate this point. You are acting for your supervisor who is on leave. All that is expected of you is to ensure that the function of the supervisor is performed. This could be ensuring that all sections of the organization produce their reports on time. What do you think is likely to happen when you start modeling your supervisor?

You are correct! You become highly critical of the performance of the persons you supervise. You keep on sending back reports to get them done properly to your standard. Meetings are convened to tell the staff about your expectations as well as your disgust or disappointment with their performance. Wow!! Modeling or acting is hard work. My question is: what is happening to the organization's goals while the emphasis is on self-centredness? Correct again! The goals of the organization will not be achieved.

When the supervisor returns, will he able to continue where he left off or will he now have to spend time building staff morale as well as assisting persons to complete the delayed reports? Wouldn't it then have been easier for all concerned, for the acting supervisor to have concentrated on the job and not on the status attached to the acting role?

Are you lost? Do not worry; there is relevance in the preceding argument to this chapter.

John is stating that he is a servant; he was sent to bear witness. Emphasis is also placed on the fact that John is not that Light. John's role was not one of status; he was happy in his humble role as the bearer of the news relating to the King of Kings and Lord of Lords.

When we forget our true role, we end up making things more difficult for all concerned as demonstrated in the previous example with the acting supervisor.

John was the forerunner of Jesus and performed well in his role, never assuming Jesus' role at any point in time. Friends, can you imagine what would have happened if John had assumed the role of Jesus as that Light? Even with John as a witness telling others that he was just the forerunner of Christ, people were still not sure what was happening. There would therefore have been chaos and people would not have been sure, who was the true Light if John had become hungry for power. Let us thank God that John remained humble and was happy to carry out the assignment given to him by God.

In our society today, how should you bear witness to the Light of Christ? You need to acknowledge Jesus as Lord of your lives and share with others your emptiness outside of Christ. You need to let others recognize that without the help of Jesus you would not have achieved the big house, the big car, the big job and the big bank account. You need to tell others that without God's grace your life would be spiritually empty.

Earlier, we spoke of demonstrating a Christ-like character and this includes being honest as a witness for Christ.

You need to let others know that it was the 'shining Light' of Jesus that saved you from drugs, the guns, poverty, divorce, the landlord and the bailiff. Tell them that you can stand as a witness today with your character as white as snow because of that Light, Jesus.

With Jesus there is no need to pretend or act. Jesus already knows everything about us. He wants you to be honest enough to bring others like yourselves to Him. People need to know about you in order to understand that Jesus loves them as they are. Come on! You need to stop being ashamed of your past. Jesus has already taken your shame on the cross and turned your darkness into light. You now are a shining light but you need to remember at all times that you are not that light; you have benefited from that light. You are now a reflection of that Light, so do not hesitate to share the good news.

– 31 –

Identifying The True Light

"That was the true Light, which gives light to every man coming into the world."

~ John 1:9 (NKJV)

In the world today, we are exposed to substitutes which are usually branded as being as good as the genuine parts. In the motor vehicle industry we have parts that are sold that will function like the genuine car parts. With jewellery we have fake gold and silver.

However, with both the car parts and jewellery we are able to tell the difference by the quality of the product. With the car parts the durability of the genuine part over time is usually the distinctive feature as some users claim that the substitutes do not last as long.

With jewellery sometimes the fake really does a good job of representing genuine gold or silver in appearance. The question, however, is: How long, will this appearance last? The fake jewellery usually changes appearance over time. In the long run fake items are more costly as they have to be replaced more frequently.

THE WORD

John makes a distinction that Jesus is the true light, Jesus is real, He is not fake. When He 'lights' our world, we receive forgiveness for our sins and we have hope of eternal life. We reap real rewards. Every human being is born in sin as a result of the fall through Adam's disobedience to God. The life of Jesus, however, gives everyone of us an opportunity to be forgiven of our sins. From the day we are born God's love shines on us and give us that light, His Son, through whom we can be saved. There is no exception to God's gift; every one of us receives the Light of Jesus. It is up to us to accept it and use the light for God's glory and our eternal life. Remember, when you receive a gift, what is important is how you use it. If you lock it away in a closet, it will be meaningless. So it is with the light of Jesus. If you do not accept the Light of Jesus, your life too will become meaningless. You will be living each day without the expectation of being united with Jesus in heaven. You still would be in darkness. This is real friends! There is a place called heaven for those who accept and use the Light of Jesus. Believe me, heaven has more to offer in beauty than anything you can imagine on the face of this earth. I am sure you will agree with me that there are some really beautiful places on this earth. These, however, cannot be compared to what God has provided for our future.

It is very important for us to read the Bible and establish a relationship with Jesus; otherwise, we could be caught by a 'fake light'. Friends, that is more costly to you than losing out on fake parts or fake jewellery. You could spend your eternity in hell. Wow!! That burns!! There is no way of escape in hell. It is important to be on your guard. How are you going to avoid the pitfall of having the wrong light shine on you? Yes! By knowing the Word of God and recognizing that there is no separation of God from His words. I sensed your question, "How many times am I going to tell you that God cannot be separated from His words?" The truth is, I am not counting.

Every time it comes home to me and grips me, I say it. Truly we serve a faithful God. I am sure we can all say amen to that.

When we buy fake parts for our cars or fake jewellery to adorn ourselves we might be able to justify our actions because our financial resources are limited. You could find yourself in a situation where your motor vehicle needs to be repaired or you want to look dazzling for an event with your limited resources. This means your choice would be restricted to either using fake or not repairing your car or attending the event.

Our action is justifiable under those circumstances because of our financial constraint. However, how do we explain to ourselves and to others reasons for not benefiting from the true Light, Jesus Christ?

We should not say we cannot afford God's Light, Jesus Christ, as the benefits are free. We do not have to pay for it and there are no traps. Whatever God says in His Word He will do it. "For God so loved the world that He gave His only begotten Son, that whoever believes in Him should not perish but have everlasting life." (John 3: 16). God did not sell us or lend us His son, He gave us. Take a few minutes to let it penetrate . . . . That's awesome isn't it?

Genuine love is given freely and so our salvation comes to us freely. I am not saying that Jesus did not pay a price. He did, with His own life, by shedding His blood for our sins.

We therefore have no excuse when we fail to benefit from the true Light of Jesus. Jesus' gift is not dependent on out economic status like other things in our lives. Since Jesus is the true light it means that there must be a fake light. Do you agree?

We should look out for the 'fake light', the devil. What he offers is temporary and a trap to steal our joy and hope of eternal life. To know whether the light is real or fake we need to measure what is happening to us against God's guidelines. Are we lured into success at any cost including stealing, coveting, gambling, dealing in drugs or lying. God's light surely doesn't shine in anything that is not upright. I am sure, in time, you will find out, if you have not already discovered, that there is a high price to pay for the devil's light and that is your soul.

Friends, it cannot be worth it, to be successful the devil's way on this earth and yet spend eternity in fire and brimstone. It is not a joke, it is written in the word of God. Please verify this information now (St. Matthew 13: 38–43).

Ensure that your light is a reflection of that 'true light'; do not wait until you are literally trapped in the flame because of your unbelief.

– 32 –

The Mystery of The Father and The Son

"He was in the world, and the world was made through Him, and the world did not know Him".

~ *John 1:10 (NKJV)*

Three important things stand out in this verse. Jesus was in the world, the world was made through Him and the world knew Him not. Sounds confusing, doesn't it? We said earlier that God created the earth in the creation story and now we are saying Jesus made the world. 'The world knew Him not,' we can all follow that part of the verse as we read in the Bible that people could not believe that Jesus was the Saviour of the world. In a real sense then, many people did not know Jesus as they rightfully should, as our Redeemer. To many persons, Jesus was just pretending to be who He was not by His reference to himself as the Son of God. The main question is:

How can the world be created by God, and now we are being told that Jesus the son of God made the world? There are a lot of mind boggling things in this study as mentioned in the introduction. Do you agree? Let us examine a passage that will help us with the answers to our question about Jesus and God. "I and my father are one" (St. John 10: 30).

We first need to understand that God is a spirit and therefore He is not restricted by time, space or form. God is not human and so in a human context when we speak about a son we are speaking about a separate human being which would be different from his father.

Have I lost you so far? No? Good, I am happy that you are following me. Do you realize that you are following me right back to the creation story? Yes, we have to start right there as God's words are unchanging. An understanding of what happened in the beginning will help us to understand reasons for God and His son being one.

In the creation story, "The Lord God formed man in His own image out of the dust of the ground and breathed into his nostrils the breath of life and man became a living-soul" (Genesis 2: 7). Later on in Genesis we read about how God made Eve and gave her to Adam as his wife. We should also remember how Adam and Eve yielded to the devil's temptation to eat of the fruit of the tree of knowledge of good and evil and were chased out of the Garden of Eden. Bear with me, this background is really important in helping us to understand the oneness of God and Jesus.

Adam and Eve were sinless and so God was able to fellowship with them on a one to one level. God visited them in the garden in the cool of the day (Genesis 3: 8).

An important point to note here is that God cannot relate to sin. Once Adam sinned, it meant that all of us as human beings were cut off from God and could not fellowship with Him as before.

THE MYSTERY OF THE FATHER AND THE SON

To fellowship with God it meant that a life would have to be sacrificed. I am sorry, I should have been more specific, a human life. Not just any human life but the life of one who had never sinned. Since all of us are born in sin because of Adam, our lives could not be used for this sacrifice. Let us reflect a little on God's Word for us to be fruitful and multiply in the creation story. As human beings, God relates to us as He has made us. He says we are to be fruitful and multiply and so in our human context a male child is representative of the father. I will substantiate my argument with reference to God's command to Abraham to offer His only son Isaac as a sacrifice. Remember, Abraham was willing to kill his son thereby proving how much He loved God. There is no human being that will ever be able to love us as God does. This means then if Abraham as a human being was willing to sacrifice his son Isaac then God who loves us so much would willingly give us His only son to die a physical death. This would enable us to receive forgiveness for our sins and ultimately experience eternal life.

In our earthly culture a child is born, grows up into an adult and assumes the role of heir or representative of the father. God, as a spirit, related to us on our human level by finding a mother to conceive Jesus through the Holy Spirit. Jesus lived a normal human life like us, from the cradle, to toddler-hood, adolescence and adulthood. Jesus, an extension of the Father (remember God is a spirit and can be in any shape or form) at the adult stage became the living sacrifice. Note, God did not prevent Jesus' death from happening like He did with Isaac for Abraham; He allowed it. The difference is that if God did not allow Jesus to die, we would still be separated from God. We would not be able to enjoy eternal life.

THE WORD

The real victory came at Jesus' resurrection; that is where our real hope lies. Let us now do a quick review of what we understand from God's Word.

God could not fellowship with us as sinners. However, since in an earthly context a son is a representative of his father, God needed a human son, His representative, to be our sacrifice so that He could relate to us on our level as human beings. God's son would therefore need human parents and He chose Mary and Joseph. That was a mouthful . . . it is indeed amazing, the power of God.

We can conclude that there is no separation between God, His Son and His Word. Understanding how Jesus could have made the world that we read about in the Old Testament and yet He was born in the New Testament was the most difficult part of that verse for me.

If I were born in the days when Jesus was on earth, I am sure I too would have a problem understanding that Jesus who is human is also deity and would be among those persons John described as, 'And the world knew Him not'.

I hope our delving into the Word of God has brought clarity in understanding more about The Father and the Son and their role in our lives. Take a few seconds to take a deep breath . . . now exhale . . .

Wow!! God is really awesome!! what a wonderful gift!! The Son of God, crucified so that we can receive eternal life . . . .

Let us all ensure that we live our lives in a manner pleasing to God so that we will be able to enjoy eternity in His presence.

– 33 –

Rejection

"He came to His own and His own did not receive Him."

~ John 1:11 (NKJV)

We are all created in the image of God. Jesus, however, came to earth as the son of Man. In other words, He was human like us.

Jesus faced hunger, thirst, despair, loneliness and betrayal like we do. Jesus did only good for the benefit of humanity but we would rather spare the life of the thief, Barabbas, rather than His.

Jesus was born amongst the animals. What an entry to earth! Despite His place of birth, what is important is that Jesus, like all of us, had to develop in the womb for nine months. He was one of us! He grew up on earth like all of us having a mother and father. Jesus had feelings, He was moved with compassion and He loved all persons. He grieved like we do; He wept at the death of Lazarus.

In the Garden of Gethsemane Jesus experienced loneliness when His disciples fell asleep and could not watch with Him. How would you have felt if you were faced with a crisis and were treated that way by your friends? Imagine, just needing some moral support and pleading with them to stay awake with you. Suddenly, you realize you are alone as they have muttered some words to you like, 'Do not worry, I am going to lie down for a while'. Your next check finds them snoring in dream land. That surely hurt! Jesus faced all of that not in the confines of His home (He had none) but in the open space, in that garden.

Jesus must have been overwhelmed by what He had to face on the cross. Imagine what it must have felt like, knowing that you were going to die for something that you did not do. We are not talking about swallowing a tablet that is fatal or about the electric chair (everything is over in a matter of seconds). We are talking about being beaten badly, having your hands nailed to a cross, and having a crown of thorn forced on your head. I know I would not want to go through all of that for something I did not do. We should all thank God for His love in bearing all of this for our sakes.

Have you ever had to suffer for something you did not do? Oh yes! You can now recall someone betraying you or doing something and blaming you for it. Most times the innocent person gets the punishment and that makes you feel helpless. Let me find out if there is anyone who is in jail innocently and is now so angry because of that experience. Stop! Right now, turn around that seemingly negative experience into one that glorifies God. Who knows? Maybe, God wants you to minister to even one person right there that you relate to very well. If you are not sure what you should be doing or learning through this experience, please ask Jesus. He has been there and done that; Jesus definitely has the answer.

Now let us talk about that kiss, the kiss of Judas the betrayer.

REJECTION

After all Jesus did for those disciples including Judas who rewarded him with betrayal. Jesus spent so much time training these disciples, caring for them genuinely, even washing their feet, and then to be handed over not for an award but to be killed, that's really hard.

How many persons are saying, "I can identify with being betrayed"? Your experience might be that of helping someone and then trusting them enough to share your secrets. That person has now revealed your secrets and everyone is talking about you. Do not worry, Jesus wants us to use the experience, whatever it might be, to His Glory. Do all the good you can without resentment, bitterness or hate. God will take care of the situation. Jesus is resurrected. He has survived the betrayal and He is saying to us today, so will you. A promise is never broken; with Jesus, you are safe.

The betrayal of Jesus and the ultimate choice of Barabbas' life over Jesus' is confirmation that Jesus was not accepted by us. Jesus, being human like us and such an exemplary one, should have been welcomed or received by us as a fellow human being. His death on the cross, however, symbolized our rejection of Him.

The willingness of humanity to allow Jesus who loved us so much to be crucified instead of a thief helps us to understand why there is so much brutal killing of each other without remorse in our society today. Some human beings, once they are against you, for whatever reason, view your life as meaningless to them. Please share the good news with any such person you know. Just show them these words . . . . Jesus died so we might learn from His experience that we need to love and protect each other as ultimately we are from one big family,

THE WORD

the family of God. There will be accountability on that day and the life we take today or plan to take could cause us to lose our own life for eternity. Stop your actions now before it is too late!

We have an amazing God who is willing to forgive our sins. All God wants us to do is to accept that we are sinners, "If we say that we have no sin we deceive ourselves and the truth is not in us" (1 John 1: 8). In addition we should confess our sins and be willing to make the changes in our lives according to His Word. God is indeed merciful so accept His offer today; do not hesitate.

− 34 −

Becoming Heirs

"But as many as received Him, to them He gave the right to become children of God, to those who believe in His name."

~ John 1:12 (NKJV)

In a biological sense we are sons of men. As explained in the previous chapter, God has made us as human beings to procreate. Children are given their father's surname and so a child then is the son or daughter of the father. Let us now examine what happens to us when we accept Jesus as our Saviour. You all know by this that I always do a review of what was previously stated where it helps in providing a better understanding. Earlier we said that Jesus, an extension of God, became His Son on earth in order to identify with human beings. Jesus was the chosen sacrifice.

To be a sacrifice representing us, Jesus had to be a human being like us in every sense of the word. He had to have an earthly mother and father like all of us. Jesus could not pay the price for our sins on the cross if He was not human like us. Our sins are human sins and so a human life was needed. Having lived on earth as a human being, Jesus died like one too.

However, unlike us, Jesus conquered death through his resurrection and then returned to heaven to God. Jesus is now interceding on our behalf and is preparing a place in heaven for us to join Him.

Be patient with me, I will make the point soon . . . . Jesus, by conquering death as a human being, has now made it possible for us to have everlasting life too. I need to remind you that there are conditions attached to enjoying eternal life; it is not automatic. If you fail to adhere to God's Word, you will instead be faced with hell eternally. This means fire and brimstone (ouch!!!) forever and ever . . . .

To receive eternal life, however, we have to be spiritual beings. That's fair! Jesus had to be human to die for our sins in order to make provisions for us spiritually. We cannot be human beings and expect to receive spiritual rewards without some transformation. Let us examine what Jesus' change of status entailed to be better able to understand our position. Jesus, God's son, had to become the son of man to work on our behalf (becoming the human sacrifice for our sins). For us to benefit from what Jesus did on our behalf we too will now have to become sons of God. Jesus moved from a spiritual being to a human being. We will have to move from being physical human beings with limited life span to spiritual beings who have eternal life.

The question is: how do we go about achieving this transformation? The answer is to believe on the Lord Jesus Christ. This includes confessing out sins, acknowledging Jesus Christ as Lord and Master and being obedient to His Word. When we do that, we are accepted by God as His heirs or children and we now will be able to enjoy eternal life with God when this phase of life ends.

Our side of the bargain is really easy. I am sure you will agree with me. We do not have to die on a cross and face the kind of betrayal Jesus did. Please note well; we will all have our cross to bear and there will be trials and struggles but luckily for us Jesus has sent us the Holy Spirit, the Comforter, who will guide us in all things. We need to remember that the Word of God must be our spiritual food daily. This is the only way to cope with our cross and to ensure that we receive the eternal reward Jesus worked so hard to provide for us.

Let us use this opportunity to remind ourselves that God cannot be separated from His Word. Therefore, both heaven and hell are real places. Our belief in and obedience to His Word determine the place we go.

– 35 –

Spiritual Rebirth

"Who were born, not of blood, nor of the will of the flesh, nor of the will of man, but of God".

~ John 1: 13 (NKJV)

Those who accept Jesus Christ as Lord of their lives receive the power to become the sons of God. Becoming the sons of God is not based on the human procreation process. As human beings, we can either plan to have a child or become sexually aroused at a point in time without thinking about the consequences of yielding to the lust of the flesh.

Whether planned or not a child is born. Children born to us as human beings are definitely sons of men. These children have one thing in common; they will all be born with a sinful nature because of Adam's sins. Sin is the hallmark of human birth. Mothers and fathers, therefore, as sinners, cannot make a decision to have children that will automatically be sons of God.

Becoming sons of God is only possible when we receive and accept Jesus as Lord of our lives. To do this we have to recognize our sinful state and the fact that this state has resulted in our separation from God. When we accept Jesus, this means that we willingly confess our sins and allow Him to take His rightful position in our lives, as Saviour and Lord.

When Jesus becomes Lord of our Lives He gives us the power to become sons of God. This power is not a physical power but a spiritual power. Through God's spiritual power we are also strengthened in our physical beings as we manifest the name of our Lord in our lives daily. I know you all agree with what I have said so far about how we become the sons of God. However, let me use some scripture references as reminders of God's promises to us throughout the remainder of this chapter. We cannot afford to forget . . . . God cannot be separated from His Word. You know I would not allow this opportunity to pass without reminding you about the power of God's Word.

To accept Jesus as Lord we first have to accept our sinful state. Note now, sin is not about some of us, sin relates to all of us. Read along with me . . . "For all have sinned and fall short of the glory of God" (Romans 3: 23). All of us have to recognize and admit our sinful state. When we do this we should feel the need to make our confession. Let's read on, "If we confess our sin, He is faithful and just to forgive us our sins, and to cleanse us from all unrighteousness" (1 John 1: 9). Once we confess, God forgives us of our sins. Jesus makes no exception, He forgives anyone who confesses: drug addict, gunman, prostitute, thief, liar, rapist . . . . any one who confesses. God's Word states, "All that the father giveth me shall come to me; and him that cometh to me I will in no wise cast out" (St. John 3: 37).

We need to now look at the proof in God's Word as it relates to Jesus' authority. Please read . . . . "For there is one God and one Mediator between God and men, the man, Christ Jesus" (1 Timothy 2: 5). Jesus mediates on our behalf and so He had to be like us. Please note what Timothy said: the man Christ Jesus not the Spirit Christ Jesus. Jesus is therefore justified to intercede on our behalf as he can identify with the human experience.

Our final reminder of the saving power of Jesus, the True Light who is preparing a place for us to enjoy eternal life is this: "Therefore He is also able to save to the uttermost those who come to God through Him (Jesus), since He always lives to make intercession for them" (Hebrew 7: 25).

What an excellent note to end on. There is no need for anyone of us to think that our lives are in too terrible a state for God to save us. Hebrews reminds us that Jesus is able to save us to the uttermost or utmost. We know that utmost means extreme. When we use the word, 'extreme', in our context as sinners, the question is: what is Jesus saying to us? Jesus is saying that no matter how far gone we are as sinners, He can save us. It does not matter if you are rejected by others and there is no one on your side. Are you about to face life imprisonment, bankruptcy, terminal illness or a future that appears hopeless? It does not matter what your circumstances are, Jesus will reach out to you and save you if you cry for help!

God's promises are guaranteed . . . . Enjoy them! We have proven this from the beginning of this book to the end.

Share the Good News of God's faithfulness daily. You will be revitalized every time you do so.

− 36 −

Conclusion

Part II has reinforced the importance of the need to accept God and His Word. Together we were reminded of an important fact that God cannot lie and what He says in His Word must come to pass. We acknowledged together the times in our lives when we gave our fellow human beings the accolades for the things they have done, failing to acknowledge God as the ultimate creator and the one who has given man knowledge to do so many things. From now on I am sure we will not make the same mistakes and will recognize God's role in man's apparent discoveries and give God the glory. Our fellow human beings will now be given their rightful place and be acknowledged by us as God's channels.

What an awesome reminder of how God identified with us and provided His Son to be our sacrifice. It was really exciting to follow the transformation that ultimately benefits us.

Let's look at it again. Jesus became human and died for us and so, was called the son of man. Jesus' resurrection gave us the hope of eternal life that could not have been ours in our sinful state. Listen to this again . . . when we believe Jesus and

THE WORD

confess our sins, He allows us to become the sons of God. We too will be able to live forever.

Part II has prepared us in a significant way to cope with the realities of the many challenges we now face or will face. The Word of God guarantees our ultimate victory. If we do not know the Word, we won't survive. On the other hand, if we know the Word but do not believe, we allow ourselves to be defeated.

Stand tall! We have reasons to be confident about each day. Go out and share the good news but remember to let your light shine in your life first so that others can see it. Think about it, the bulb in your room provides light in the room although it reflects elsewhere. A very bright light in your room will provide a better source of lighting for your room as well as surrounding areas. So too with our lives, when we shine as we should for God, others benefit from the light.

Shine brightly!!!! . . . God loves you.

God Bless You All.

www.ingramcontent.com/pod-product-compliance
Lightning Source LLC
Chambersburg PA
CBHW080433110426
42743CB00016B/3155